LET'S HAVE LUNCH

Conversation, Race and Community; Celebrating 20 years of the Presbyterian Inter-Racial Dialogue

STEPHEN McCUTCHAN

PRIMIX
PUBLISHING
THE WRITE CHOICE

Primix Publishing
11620 Wilshire Blvd
Suite 900, West Wilshire Center, Los Angeles, CA, 90025
www.primixpublishing.com
Phone: 1-800-538-5788

Published by Primix Publishing: 02/15/2024

ISBN: 979-8-89194-052-9(sc)
ISBN: 979-8-89194-053-6(e)

Library of Congress Control Number: 2024900921

CONTENTS

CONVERSATIONS AND COMMUNITY

CHAPTER 1

I want to invite you to a conversation about race and racism as we experience it in this country. This conversation can be about race on a national level and include the decisions leading to the institution of slavery, the experiences of being bought and sold, the promise of freedom for slaves, the impact of Jim Crow Laws, the civil rights movement, and the struggle of the Caucasian society to adjust to a diverse and equal community. It also can be on a personal level about how you feel about race and racism. It can include prejudice, fear of differences, sexual myths, and violence. I want to ask you, however, to share in a conversation from the perspective of community, in this case the church community and the city of Winston-Salem. Other churches and other denominations have engaged in this conversation, but I want to invite you to a conversation about how a group of Presbyterians chose to engage in this dialogue.

This story begins in 1992. It was a difficult year with respect to race relations both national and locally. Nationally the Rodney King decision exonerating the police officers who had been videoed beating an apparently defenseless Mr. King during the riots in Los Angeles had raised tensions all across the nation.

Those tensions were exacerbated in Winston-Salem by three public incidents. An African American woman, Sheila Epps McKellar, had been arrested on drug charges, handcuffed, gagged, and thrown into a cell at the local jail. Whether she vomited with the gag on or for some other reason, the woman died while in the cell unattended. The second incident was the case of an African American transient, Carlos Leo Stoner, whose body was discovered under a bridge. When examined, it was discovered that his genitals had been removed and stuffed in his mouth. Historically this was an act with specific racial connotations. Four white men were arrested for the murder. The third incident involved four African American teenage boys in East Winston who discovered a road grader with its keys in the ignition and chose to take a joy ride. When they were confronted by a white police officer, Lieutenant Tise, they chose to run over his car, crushing him to death.

Whether you lived in Winston-Salem in 1992 or not, try to either recall or place yourself in the city at that time. If you as an individual citizen of this city were feeling the tension of these and other incidents, what could you do that might make a positive contribution to healing the tensions in your city?

That was the challenge that confronted three Presbyterian ministers, two African American and one Caucasian, who pastored churches within the city. None of them were native to the city. Carlton Eversley arrived in 1982 as a Baptist pastor but became Presbyterian so that he could accept the pastorate of Dellabrook Presbyterian Church. Stephen McCutchan, the Caucasian, had come from a pastorate in Pennsylvania in 1983 to become pastor of Highland Presbyterian Church. Samuel Stevenson, a second-career pastor, having left the field of mental health to attend seminary, came to Winston in 1990 to become pastor at Grace Presbyterian Church.

As Presbyterians are inclined to do when deciding on important decisions, they chose to meet for lunch. They deliberately chose to meet in a downtown restaurant, Giselles, that was managed by an African American businessman. Being relatively recent to the city, they did not have any particular influence in the city structures. Like you as you consider what you would have done, so they were infected by racism, shaped by their own biographies, and shocked by the events that were troubling their adopted city.

They knew each other as Presbyterian colleagues but not with any depth that could remove the vague feelings of distrust that were natural to the association of races within the community. Later, when they became good friends, Sam would confess to his response when Steve had invited him to lunch a few months earlier when Sam first came to the city. You go to lunch with your white colleagues so that they can feel good about inviting you, but you don't expect anything significant to come out of the relationship. Now they were again at lunch, this time including Carlton, and the issues before them would test the bonds of friendship.

What separated them was the stain of racism that shaped their respective histories. What connected them was that they were all three Presbyterian pastors. The question before them was whether their faith, which called them to be ambassadors of reconciliation, could transcend the divisions that plagued their society. Even more than whether they could rise above such divisions was the question of whether they could provide some leadership that would contribute to healing within Winston-Salem. If you had been one of them, how would you have felt as you first arrived for lunch?

As the three pastors ate their sandwiches and drank their soft drinks, they focused on who they were. They recognized that while they were not in a position to effect major changes to heal the city, they were all three pastors drawn by a faith that focused on community and overcoming, in their terms, the sins that separated them. They had the freedom and opportunity to address the people of their churches every week and guide them in a journey towards wholeness. In religious terms, if the people of their churches took steps towards overcoming the divisions of racism, they would have a witness to make to the city as a whole.

So on that fall day in a downtown restaurant in Winston-Salem in 1992, the idea was formed to create the Presbyterian Interracial Dialogue. Their first commitment was to draw a representative group from their three congregations that would educate themselves with respect to the history of racism, draw on the resources of their Christian faith, and build a sense of community across racial lines. They agreed to begin with forty people, twenty from Highland, the larger church, and ten each from Grace and Dellabrook.

The first meeting took place at Grace Presbyterian on November 15, 1992, at 4 p.m. Forty people gathered under the guidance of their pastors. They were all Presbyterians but, separated by race, many of them were strangers to each other. Their pastors each shared what had led them to convene the meeting and their goal of improving race relations in the city beginning with their own churches. Then, in small mixed groups led by the pastors, the individuals introduced themselves. Each was asked to state one way faith shaped his or her view of the racial tension within the city. Following that sharing, they were asked to speak to one hope they held for the dialogue. The third round began to explore personal biography. Each was asked to share four to six of the most important events that had shaped his or her life.

When they had regathered as a total group, the pastors brought to their attention the types of events noted that were connected with race. As one participant noted, "Caucasians don't have to know blacks to survive, while blacks have to know whites to survive." Then she said "I don't see it as my responsibility to teach whites, but my faith says I should care." The vision of faith led her beyond her immediate feelings.

The group decided that they would continue to meet on a bi-monthly basis with the second meeting to be held at Highland. At that meeting, the group began to probe the impact of racism at a more visceral level. Each was asked to complete the following four sentences: "Racism feels like ….", Racism looks like ….", Racism sounds like ….", and Racism in the church looks like …." The meetings included an experience of worship that reminded the participants of the common faith that held them together.

By the third meeting, the group began to explore what African Americans have to offer the Presbyterian Church and what Caucasians have to offer the Presbyterian Church. Participants were invited to draw names and get together socially between meetings to deepen their friendships. While this was beneficial for some, it was discovered that these more intimate meetings were uncomfortable for others. The combination of human shyness and historic racial separation is not easily overcome by good intentions.

Once you had some initial conversations, how would you proceed to build a deeper understanding of the impact of racism and how to respond to it? These initial members of the Dialogue determined that they needed to study the history of racism in our society in order to build their understanding. The group benefited from the willingness of one of its participants, Dr. Pauline Fulton, to guide the group in the study of *Before the Mayflower* by Dr. Lerone Bennet, Jr. Building on that historic foundation, they next chose *Race Matters* by Dr. Cornel West that probed the complexity of racism in our current society. This was followed by *Two Nations* by Andrew Hacker, which confronted them with the perspective of race as seen by the behavior of both white and black citizens.

Would you have spent that much time studying together, or would you have grown restless wondering where this was leading? A phrase made popular during the Civil Rights movement is that it is important to not only "talk the talk but also to walk the walk." As the group would discover, "walking the walk" can sometimes be uncomfortable.

BUILDING THE COMMUNITY

CHAPTER 2

While our conversation is focused on a community of Presbyterians, there have been past and continuing efforts by other churches to engage in interracial conversation. Several churches have reached out to churches of other races, had meals and worship together, joined in mission projects, and engaged in other activities. St. Anne's Episcopal Church was even founded as a deliberately interracial church.

Neither was it the first effort at racial conversation among Presbyterians. Sometimes these efforts were led by the clergy, but frequently in the Presbyterian Church cutting edge efforts at reaching out beyond the boundaries of a single congregation were led by the women's groups of these churches. Several years prior to the initiation of the Presbyterian Interracial Dialogue, the women's organizations of Dellabrook and Trinity Presbyterian churches had reached out to each other in fellowship. Soon they augmented their efforts and convinced their churches to come together once a year in worship and follow with a picnic.

Knowing that tradition, if you were a member of Trinity Presbyterian or their pastor, and you heard about what was happening in the Presbyterian Inter-Racial Dialogue, wouldn't it be natural to pursue the possibility of becoming part of the Dialogue? Late in 1993, the pastor of Trinity Presbyterian, Stewart Ellis, began making inquiries about that possibility.

Already having studied together for a year, the Dialogue of forty had talked about expanding their relationships to include other members of their churches. It seemed to them incongruous to be studying about how to break down barriers that separate and not be open to including more people. Besides, they reasoned, if the original impetus for their group was to have a positive impact on the city, wasn't it natural to want to at least begin by being open to more Presbyterians. So, in January, 1994, Trinity Presbyterian became a member of the Dialogue.

It's a funny thing about community—if you are open to it, it can become contagious. Parkway Presbyterian, who was in the midst of a search for a new pastor, was being guided in the interim process by the Reverend John Wilkerson. As they were exploring the direction of their ministry in preparation for calling a new pastor, they expressed an interest in being more involved in the community around them. John made inquiry as to the possibility of Parkway also becoming part of the Dialogue. In May, 1994, the Dialogue now had five Presbyterian churches. Later when they called Dan Wilkers to be the pastor of Parkway, he shared that knowing Parkway was part of an inter-racial dialogue was a positive factor in accepting the call.

This new configuration, however, did raise an important question for the Dialogue. From its inception, there was a sensitivity to maintaining a balance within the Dialogue. You will recall that in the original forty participants, twenty were from a predominantly Caucasian church, Highland, and twenty were drawn from the two smaller African American churches, Dellabrook and Grace. Now there were two African American churches and three Caucasian churches.

This led to the Dialogue deliberately seeking out the remaining African American Presbyterian Church in Winston-Salem. In January 1995 Lloyd Presbyterian, the second oldest African American church in Winston-Salem, became part of the Dialogue. Lloyd's presence in the Dialogue is an excellent example of Paul's insistence that no part of the body can ever say, "I have no need of you."

Lloyd was a unique participant from several perspectives. When the conversation began as to Lloyd's participation, it is probably fair to say that though the Caucasian pastors of the Dialogue knew about Lloyd, none of them had ever visited the church and most of their members did not even know of its existence.

According to Lloyd's stated clerk, the church had its birth when a man named George Wills invited a small group to begin to gather for worship in a school house in 1870. At that time, there was a small community of African Americans who were allowed to *hear* worship at First Presbyterian as long as they sat behind some panels that shielded them from the view of the main congregations. When these people learned of the gathering at the school building, they began to explore the idea of joining and soon they wanted to build a church on the property where the schoolhouse stood. It should be noted that First Presbyterian not only supported them in this effort but became a strong supporter of Lloyd at various times in their history.

There is a sign in front of the church that also gives credit to northern missionaries who supported the establishment of the church. The story is that these missionaries helped establish both this church in Winston-Salem and one in Charlotte at about the same time. Reflective of their commitment, they suggested the name Lloyd after William Lloyd Garrison who had fought so hard against slavery in this country. Perhaps it was those seeds planted that shaped the DNA of a church that has always been committed to the larger community and to the dignity of each human being.

In the 1870s, the people did not have the resources to hire someone to build their church, so they decided to build it themselves. The women of the church built the lower part of the building and the men built the upper half. Drawing from pictures they had seen of Gothic cathedrals, they tried to replicate the design in wood. This design became known as "Carpenter Gothic." The notched and pegged pews of that original church are still used by the congregation. Later some members of this church moved to form Grace Presbyterian.

From its inception, Lloyd has been a church interested in the larger community. In the '60's, meetings were frequently held at Lloyd during the Civil Rights movement. For the Dialogue to work to revitalize their ministry seemed appropriate.

During their 125-year history, they have only had three full time pastors and their last pastor, State Alexander, retired in 1968. Not infrequently, there had been discussions in presbytery as to the viability of the church and whether it should be closed down. It was probably because of the fierce determination of their clerk of Session, Mr. Patterson, that the church continued to function. Near the close of the pastorate of State Alexander, Katy Reed, a Caucasian colleague of the Dialogue pastors, began to serve as their moderator and supply preacher. It was under her leadership that the church expressed an interest in being part of the Dialogue.

As Paul said in 1 Corinthians 12:22, ". . .the members of the body that seem to be weaker are indispensable. . ." The members of the Dialogue began to dream about how they might support and help with the revitalization of this part of the Body of Christ. In June of 1995, they engaged in conversation with the Presbytery with respect to revitalizing the ministry at Lloyd. Then, in accord with the Session of Lloyd church, on November 11, 1995 volunteers from the Dialogue churches gathered to do some minor repairs and lots of painting. Thanks to some excellent carpenter work by members of Parkway, Grace, and Highland, they also were able to bring a new look to the church's basement, which would later serve as a location for some very creative ministry.

In addition to this work, Sam Stevenson, Laura Spangler, and Carlton Eversley began to try to draft a job description to submit to the presbytery that would provide for a part time pastor at Lloyd for support. Reflective of the Christian faith, that which appeared to be near death began to breathe new life. In July 1997, Laura Spangler was appointed moderator of the Lloyd session and Bill Shouse, a commissioned lay pastor from Grace began leading worship there.

When the General Assembly met in Charlotte in 1998, about twenty-five commissioners took advantage of the opportunity to come to Winston-Salem to see what was happening at Lloyd.

In August 1998, in addition to being moderator of their session, Laura Spangler was called to be their stated supply. Under Laura's leadership, the church continued their community involvement. An example of the new life that was being breathed into Lloyd was a ministry initiated by Laura and Elder Estella McFadden. In 1998, Laura and Estella began a neighborhood Bible study in which "the poor (had the) good news brought to them." (Matthew 11:5). This Bible study, which reached out to the poor and the homeless in the church's neighborhood was strengthened when some women from First Presbyterian decided to both join the study and bring food to feed the participants. Four to seven women have been coming every week since then, bringing enough food to feed 30 or more people.

Strengthening Lloyd's ministry was the arrival of Clarisse Durnell in 1999. Clarisse was an educator who, in addition to strengthening the youth program of the Dialogue and assisting Grace and Dellabrook with their educational ministries, became an active presence at Lloyd. A major focus of her work was the development of the Helping Hands tutorial program that reached out to the children in the neighborhood. This drew on volunteers from Trinity, Highland, Parkway, and Grace Churches.

In June 2000, Parkway Presbyterian youth teamed up with youth from Messiah Moravian and Epiphany Lutheran to build a playground at Lloyd. This was part of an urban experience for youth created by these three churches. They also spent their evenings at Winston-Salem State learning about their city.

Advent is a time of expectation for the birth of new hope. The Lloyd session, after a season of prayer, decided to serve a catered meal to worshippers on the third Sunday of each month. The positive results of this venture in faith was almost immediate. Attendance at worship tripled as people opened themselves to food for the body and the soul. The worship service came alive with clapping and singing and the joyful influx of children.

The second new event born at Lloyd during that time was an outreach program under the guidance of Sister Ella Pomeroy. In her search for a location to center her outreach to the homeless, she found the renovated basement at Lloyd the right place to gather people for fellowship, prayer, clothing, haircuts, shoeshines, sewing, food, notary service, arts and crafts, and devotions. In a variety of ways, Lloyd became a beacon of hope and compassion for the often forgotten of our society.

This effort continued to expand in late 2003. After some members had participated in the anti-racism training by IDR, the session of Lloyd voted to be intentional about being a multicultural congregation and building a diverse community of faith. As the neighborhood changed, the apartments across the street from Lloyd were increasingly filled with Hispanic families, so the tutoring program became another ministry across culture and language..

In 2001, Harold Wingert and friends of First Presbyterian of Winston-Salem helped Lloyd open a door on the south side of the building and construct a ramp for the handicapped. Adam Eberle, of Highland Presbyterian focused his Eagle Scout project on landscaping and building benches for the grounds at the church. The Parkway youth chose to help with projects at Lloyd several times over the years.

In 2007, Lloyd faced a major crisis. Major renovations to their building were necessary and the cost was estimated to be around $208,000. To be a connectional church for Presbyterians means more than providing financial support to a hierarchy. Presbyterians believe that they are part of one body and when a part of the body hurts, it is an opportunity to reach out in support. Pat Toole, a member of the Covenant Class at First Presbyterian church, heard of the challenge for Lloyd and offered to help lead a fund raising effort. She was assisted by Eleanor Godfrey and Lorraine Thompson from the same class. They formed a committee of representatives from area Presbyterian churches, searched out grants, held fundraisers, and believed it could be done. The Dialogue offered to join with First church in raising the funds and to commit an initial $1,000 towards the project. In about one year over $250,000 had been raised and Lloyd completed their renovation without a loan or debt being incurred. As Laura said, "I was there to pastorally encourage hope in what God can do for renewal. We still thank the Lord for this miracle."

In 2010, Lloyd continued to reach out in innovative ministry. They developed eleven raised garden beds filled with greens, lettuce, spinach, peas, carrots, Swiss chard, potatoes, cabbage, broccoli, and strawberries to contribute to the healthy diet of the neighborhood. Then in May

2011, Lloyd was the focal point for the Dialogue sponsored Spring for Haiti Outdoor Fair and Benefit.

In its 137th year, Lloyd received a 2011 Heritage Award from Preserve historic Forsyth in cooperation with the city of Winston-Salem for an institution showing extraordinary work for their renovations and preservation.

As Paul also said in 1 Corinthians 12:26, ". . .if one member is honored, all rejoice together with it." It wasn't the *little engine that could*, but *the little church that could*. Logic would have suggested that Lloyd would close in the latter part of the 20th century, but God had other plans.

Two years after the Dialogue began, there were three predominantly black churches and three predominantly white churches, and this balance would continue until the present.

At another level, the issue of balance became a part of some deeper challenges that are part of any attempt at building community among the churches. You may recognize a major challenge when you consider that the combined membership of the participating Caucasian churches in 1998 was approximately 1400 members and the combined membership of the predominantly African American churches was about 400 members. This was surfaced in a rather difficult exchange that occurred among members of the Dialogue during one of their discussions in September 1998.

The question was raised by several white members of the Dialogue as to why fewer and fewer Blacks seemed to be participating in the meetings. Ms. P of the Parkway Presbyterian Church referenced the positive experiences the Presbyterian Women's groups of Trinity and Dellabrook had had, and suggested that the all six of our churches needed to find other ways to have shared experiences. Dr. Eversley reacted rather strongly pointing out that because of the numerically fewer number of blacks in the participating churches, there was a danger of exhausting them because they also had many other responsibilities in their respective churches.

Later Eversley wrote a letter commenting on the exchange. "My pastoral intuition that Ms. P was upset by my statements was born out by a later phone call from Inis (Johnson – a member of Dellabrook.). Even the fact that I couldn't deal with that after the meeting highlights my point, because I was rushing to a fiftieth birthday party for Alderman (and Dellabrook elder) Fred Terry.

"Finally, we have to be honest to admit that for certain groups of African-Americans, the weekend are a refuge from whites, who usually supervise their employment. I think our Dialogue will grow with blacks who are not burned out at either the ecclesiastical or racial level. That can be cultivated and nurtured, but only if we all understand each other, no matter how painfully that understanding is purchased."

As the gatherings continued over the twenty years of our history, there were frequent meetings in which the number of Caucasians present outnumbered the African Americans by two or even three to one. For many Caucasians, this was frustrating because their whole purpose in being part of these experiences was to build both understanding and friendships. Part of the explanation was the unequal number of absolute participants as mentioned. However, as the concern was discussed among those involved, another learning surfaced for the Caucasian participants.

From the beginning, there had been the unspoken assumption among many Caucasians, that African Americans would be delighted and enthusiastic to be part of the Dialogue. What they had neglected to factor in was the daily emotional cost to African Americans of interaction with Caucasians in our society. As some African Americans would eventually acknowledge, all week long they were interacting with the white society, always being alert to how they were being received and when the response of both individuals and institutions was being affected by their skin color rather than their personhood. While they were pleased that their church was active in the Dialogue, there were many times when they felt too drained to attend one more meeting, especially one that focused on the issue of race. Theoretically, talking was important in building community and deepening understandings among the races, but Dialogue meetings were a choice where their weekly interactions were a necessity.

After the first blush of enthusiasm moved into long range efforts, the Caucasian congregations also found the constant challenge of encouraging participation of their membership. If the major drain on their energy was not the sensitivity to racial interactions as it was for their African American participants, still there were many other drains on their energy through the week, so they too chose to allow others to engage in dialogue while they offered silent support. As more than one pastor commented, my congregation brags to others that their church is part of the Dialogue but when it comes to being part of an event, they choose not to be present. For the Caucasian participants, sometimes it was not just an issue of energy level. Sometimes it was family obligations – sports, etc., and sometimes it was discomfort in openly interacting around the issue of race.

Individuals from both the Caucasian and African American community began with the Dialogue but decided that they were uncomfortable for various reasons and chose to drop out.

J, a lawyer who attended the first two meetings, wrote a letter explaining why he would not return to the group. He said he was offended by some of the comments made by Carlton Eversley in the early discussions. Among other comments, J said, referring to Reverend Eversley, "His comments exhibit a basic distrust of me as a person, a need to prove myself not because of who I am, but because I am white. . . The time is long past for this type of reverse prejudice which only continues the racial division which I believe Mr. Eversley unknowingly promotes to generate emotionally supportive responses from his *followers* and sympathizers."

After also complaining about Eversley's description of a black nativity scene in his church, J continued, "I am also uncomfortable with any group that attributes the term racism to only one side of the racial fence . . . That is a totally unacceptable concept. Those factors of racial division exist in both races. A refusal to recognize this only deepens the differences and makes peaceful compromises more difficult." He concludes his letter by saying, "I have had to hear most of my life how guilty I should feel for what unknown ancestors of mine did to unknown ancestors of today's blacks. I was not there. I did not do it and I do not feel guilty. I do feel anger towards those who seek to control me by trying to make me feel guilty. I refuse to let anyone, white or black, attempt to control me emotionally."

How would you respond upon hearing J's comments. For the clergy who were leading the group, the saddest thing about J's letter was not the feelings he expressed but that we had not developed the trust in which such feelings could be shared within the group. While Steve McCutchan did respond to his letter, and Luellen Curry, the wife of Reverend Eversley who knew J professionally, also responded to him, J did not return to the discussions and an opportunity to grow in our understanding of each other was lost.

J was not the only one who found experiences within the group disturbing to them personally. Among others, one African American woman wrote of her choice to not continue her participation. In part, she said, "Without question *Before the Mayflower* and *Race Matters* (the two books that had been part of our initial study together) probe deeply and passionately into the collective experience, behavior, and psyche of my own race, and both provide considerable insights to anyone seeking to understand how where I have been informs who and where I am.

"However, if race relations are problematic in our nation, in our city, and in our community of faith, they are not problematic merely as a result of my American story but they are so as a result of yours, too. I am frankly therefore disheartened that, to my knowledge, the Dialogue has yet to undertake a formal study or engage relevant texts which critically examine how where you have been informs where (and who) you are. And so I struggle (I really do struggle) to clarify for myself how genuine understanding, healing, and wholeness can evolve if half of our mutual experience is left unexamined."

If you reflect on it, both letters are almost mirror reflections of the other and a plea for greater understanding and sensitivity to the people involved. While neither person was willing to stay with the Dialogue, they both contributed to helping everyone understand the incredible complexity of the task before us.

In October of 1999, in a slightly whimsical article in the newsletter that also reveals the challenge of encouraging participation from the churches, there were listed ten reasons that people gave for not participating in the Dialogue.

1. Dialogue is all talk and no action.
2. It is about a black problem, and I am white.
3. It is a white organization, and I'm black.
4. I'm tired of touch feely sessions.
5. I deal with white (black) people all week long, and I don't want to do it on the weekend.
6. Wilkers (or Stevenson, Spangler, Ellis, McCutchan, Eversley, Henderson) is pushing an agenda I'm not interested in.
7. Eversley is too controversial.
8. What's a Presbyterian Inter-racial Dialogue?
9. I don't think race should be emphasized. We should all just love each other.
10. It upsets me too much to talk about it?

The article ended with the question, "What is your excuse?"

Even as the Dialogue struggled with these issues and deepened their understanding of the complexity of racism in our society, one of the extra benefits that was discovered was the strengthening relationship among the clergy of the participating churches. Bound by professional ties but constrained by other pressures and realities, while they knew each other, it was in regular meetings to plan events for the Dialogue that trusting friendships developed. Sometimes there were surprising connections of which they had been unaware. For example, Sam Stevenson and Stuart Ellis discovered that they each had been married on the same day and hour as the other and both couples *spent their first night in a Holiday Inn.* This led to a yearly sharing of an anniversary celebration with their spouses.

The clergy also learned that they could resource each other in events that had nothing to do with the Dialogue itself. From resources for officer training, to combining resources in order to respond to a person who had come for assistance, to social events and assistance in church projects, they became friends.

The clergy also found the value of continuing to build their relationship with each other and to feed each other in a different way. Sam Stevenson began sharing a monthly meal with Dr. Al Winn, father-in-law of Stuart Ellis. Dr. Winn, was a retired Presbyterian pastor who in addition to having pastored some major churches, also had been President of Louisville Presbyterian Seminary and Moderator of the Presbyterian Church. Again at a lunch, Dr. Winn suggested a lectionary support group for the clergy that gathered monthly to examine the Scriptures upon which they would preach.

When the United Way, responding to the rising racial tension in the city, convened a committee, one of their first acts was to survey what was already happening in the city. They discovered that there were almost 100 groups who identified part of their purpose as that of improving racial relations in the city. Over the next decade, most of those groups ceased to exist. You might wonder why the Dialogue was the exception.

Many factors can be identified but a very significant factor was the continuity of the Presbyterian clergy who helped form the Dialogue. For the first 14 years of the Dialogue's existence, the participating Presbyterian churches experienced little change in their pastorates. Even today, in 2012, even though some have retired, they still reside in Winston-Salem and offer their support for the Dialogue and its mission.

During these 20 years, the pastors have not only worked together but also played together and enjoyed each other. You can catch a flavor of their relationship in public remarks made at significant events.

At Carlton Eversley's 20th anniversary celebration of his ministry, Steve McCutchan was invited to speak. His remarks were as follows:

> Three minutes was what I was told
> To speak of a friendship twenty years old
>
> Now it's true that each of us has a different mother
> But I am proud to speak of Carlton as my brother

We have walked together along the way
Fighting the battle and having our say

I baptized his daughter and he prayed for my wife
We have fought for justice and the healing of strife

In 92, Sam Stevenson, Carlton and I
Spoke of racial tension and the need to try

To form a dialogue in our community
That would demonstrate the Gospel triunity

Now our churches number six
Who seek to demonstrate a Pentecostal mix

Of love that has a word to speak
Of the better world that we all do seek

That race was something God did create
So that variety and differences people might appreciate

Now we all know that white men can't jump very high
But Carlton has often been my inspiration to try

My three minutes is probably done and its time to shut my trap
So I offer Carlton my love in this poor attempt at a white man's rap

At the occasion of Steve McCutchan's retirement, the Dialogue held a party and Dan Wilkers offered the following reflection:

McCutchan's Done

From preaching and from teaching,
From yelling and from screeching,
McCutchan's done.

From pushing and motivating,
From ecclesial aggravating,
McCutchan's done.

From stewardship berating,
From watching and from waiting,
McCutchan's done

From daily office hours,
From those who like their powers,
McCutchan's done.

From constant renovation,
From far too little vacation,
McCutchan's done.

From worrying about members,
From fanning dying embers,
McCutchan's done.

From meetings with the staff,
From insufficient laughs,
McCutchan's done.

From meetings with committees,
From baptizing itty-bitty's,
McCutchan's done.

From funerals and from weddings,
From occasional forgettings,
McCutchan's done.

From compulsion and from oversight,
From worrying when the money's tight,
McCutchan's done.

From retreats for planning,
From age group spanning,
McCutchan's done.

From endless complaints,
From the bitching of the saints,
McCutchan's done.

To stories yet to write,
To not getting too uptight,
To walking in the light,
To working for what's right,
McCutchan's never done.

To Sandy's wishlist, "hon,"
To do what must be done.
To new battles to be won,
To new ways of having fun,
McCutchan's just begun.

The increased communication among the congregations of the Dialogue expanded in December 1994 with the launching of a regular newsletter. The design of the newsletter, with an iconic symbol of a city skyline reflected in a mirror image of both day and night, was published about six times a year. A three column, two sided sheet of paper made it easy for the churches to reproduce it and include it as a bulletin insert. In addition to announcing upcoming events, the newsletter frequently shared insights as to what was being learned and the challenges being faced by the community. The result was that even those who were not regular participants in the Dialogue were continually updated on the work of the Dialogue. Not infrequently this led to people who were not normally active choosing to be present for special events sponsored by the Dialogue.

The thrust towards openness to and a desire to understand more about those who were different in our community continued to expand in ways that had not originally been anticipated. When 9/11 occurred, for example, relationships with the Muslim community had already been established. Joint worship services and other events could be quickly arranged and potential tension among our communities was lessened.

In a similar fashion, as the Hispanic immigrant population grew in Winston-Salem, the Dialogue was able to reach out to El Buen Pastor, the Presbyterian Hispanic church that had been established in Winston-Salem. The new Hispanic pastor, Rosa Miranda, was invited to preach at one of our Dialogue worship services.

As the Dialogue became involved in efforts to build Habitat for Humanity houses, it was natural to include the Jewish and Muslim faith communities and to have Hispanic participants that expanded the diversity of our community.

All of this was consistent with the initial Mission Statement that the group had accepted in June, 1993, a little more than six months after their initial conversations.

"It is the mission of this group, bonded by Christian love and caring . . .

- To begin to break down barriers which stand between us as black people and white people.
- To share knowledge and experiences which will enable us to know an understand one another.
- To become an active, viable witness of Christian love in our community.

Over the history of the Dialogue, there would be revisions to the mission statement, but this was the initial hunger that drew them together. Remembering the stresses that existed in 1992, and the continuing challenge of racism in our society, how would you respond to being part of such a community?

SOCIAL EVENTS AND BUILDING FRIENDSHIPS

CHAPTER 3

B oth study and action come easier when you have also been able to enjoy each other in social events. The clergy who were designing these first experiences knew that you could come and participate in a discussion without developing new friendships. People who sat across from you in the discussion might become acquaintances, but the development of friendships required more interaction. What would be your first steps in helping people move beyond intellectual exchange and begin to build friendships?

The most natural setting for developing friendships is your home. Many white and black people have not experienced being invited to the home of a member of another race. Think about where contact is made between people of different races. The Z Smith Reynolds Foundation study of *Racial Attitudes of North Carolinians* in 1993, and reinforced by The *Study of Race Relations in Forsyth County* in 1997, suggested that the most frequent contact between races is when they are shopping, the second is at work, less but some contact where they recreate and where they live and sad to say the least contact where they worship. Does that match with your experience?

If you think about that, where people have the most opportunity to share perceptions of reality is where they talk least. Hoping personal friendships would develop but not wanting to artificially force an exchange of home visits, the clergy who were designing these initial meetings came up with a mid-way step. As a way to assist people in becoming better acquainted in a social way, at each meeting they placed people's names in a hat and paired them up with the request that before the next meeting the partners would meet for lunch or some other social way. While this was effective and fun for some, it was discovered that it was uncomfortable for others. This was especially true when the pair was among some of the older members and the pairing was a man and a woman.

In some cases, these efforts to build friendships had some surprising results. One Caucasian member, Betty Grigg, and one African American member, Inis Johnson, discovered they were reared in the same small town, were both teachers, and had several other shared life experiences but had never met. They delighted in crossing the divide and discovering a new friendship.

Sam Stevenson, believing that integrity required the clergy to also reach out in the same way that was requested of lay members, came to Steve McCutchan with a specific proposal. If, he suggested, we were really going to develop a real friendship, we needed to plan to spend some more time together. He proposed that he and Steve begin to meet for breakfast at least a couple of times a month and see what would develop.

They deliberately chose the Trenwest Restaurant (later called Jimmy the Greek) because they felt it was off the beaten path and unlikely that they would be interrupted by colleagues and other friends. This began 18 years of twice monthly breakfasts that resulted in many shared adventures, some of which will be mentioned later in this history. One ironic sidebar to this experience was that for at least fifteen years they were served by the same waitress, Debbie.

At one point, Debbie approached them and asked if either of them were willing to conduct a wedding for one of her waitress colleagues. When they checked their calendars, Sam Stevenson was available to conduct some pre-marital counseling and Steve McCutchan was available to conduct the wedding in the couple's trailer. It was a unique matching for all involved.

Early on the Dialogue discovered the frustration of a divided city and the uneasiness that people felt in venturing into sections of the city with which they were unfamiliar. It was not uncommon when the Dialogue event was held on the East side of the city for more African Americans to attend and when it was on the West side, the comfort level shifted towards the Caucasians. As the Dialogue held more events in their respective churches, more people felt comfortable in attending because they were no longer confused about directions to these churches.

One of the early successful events to bring members of the congregations together was an ice cream social. The first Dialogue sponsored ice cream social was held at Highland on July 17, 1994 and drew more than 150 people from the congregations. Recognizing that Presbyterians had a fondness for food, the Dialogue also began a yearly summer picnic beginning in 1996 alternating from one side of the city to the other each year.

Both picnics and ice cream socials have become regular events over the twenty years of the Dialogue. It quickly became a tradition to add a hymn sing to the event. As churches through the ages have discovered, music and food are shared events that transcend the divisions created by our society.

While several people were capable and willing to lead the body in song, a new dimension to our singing began when Sally Morris became the music director at Parkway Presbyterian. Soon we were singing not only music emphasized by our respective traditions but also music drawn from the international community of faith. We were tasting the oneness of the Body of Christ around the world.

In June 1999, Parkway expanded the social experience by inviting families to come together for a family fun day. Again there was food but also games, music, skits, etc. This time it was an experience of children, youth, and adults.

Members began looking for community events in which they might share. In December of 1994, they arranged to see the movie, Sankofa, and then gathered on January 15 at Grace to discuss the movie. They also began to invite the other congregations to special events in their own congregation. Grace invited the Dialogue churches to some musical events at Grace in February 1995 and Trinity invited the churches to a discussion of the video, "The Dream Long Deferred."

The Black Theater Festival provided opportunity for socializing among Dialogue members, as did certain art events. In 1997, the Dialogue met at SECCA to view the showing of Reconstruction by William Christenberry that explored the Klan movement in North Carolina.

On February 26, 2000, the Dialogue met at the Visitor's Center in Old Salem to hear from Dr. Mel White who had done extensive research on various ethnic groups throughout the triad including that of Moravian-Germans, Scotch-Irish, African, and English. He made a presentation about the Walker's Appeal, a powerful anti-slavery statement written by a man from Wilmington, NC that affected laws throughout the south. Then they visited St. Phillips Church, the second colored cemetery, and Happy Hills Garden community to understand part of the local African American history.

The Parkway Men's group invited the men of the Dialogue to an event in March of 2001 and The Grace Men's group reciprocated in May of 2001 for a cookout. This continues on an irregular basis.

You might think that all of these efforts to build relationships were just a bunch of warm-fuzzy actions that were of less importance to the purpose of the Dialogue than the actions that were taken. *The Study on Race Relations in Forsyth County* released by the United Way provides perspective on the critical importance of building these relationships.

They counted over 100 different groups who in some way or another were trying to address the racial problem in this city.

As "D" Smith of the Urban League said after hearing that report: "If there are that many groups working on the problem of racism, how come we aren't making more progress?"

Understanding this enigma was helped by the Z Smith Reynolds Foundation commissioned poll of 1993 concerning racial attitudes in NC. When we deal with race relations, we are dealing with matters of perception. We act on what we believe is true even if the facts don't back us up It is clear from the survey that the perceptions of Blacks and Whites differ greatly.

It can be summed up in the words of a familiar quotation that hung on one of the pastor's walls: "I know you think you understand what you thought I said but I am not sure you realize that what you heard is not what I meant." Communication is based on understanding. Understanding requires clarifying our perceptions.

For example, if you believed that whites and blacks generally get equal justice from the system of justice in our society, as do 60% of the whites surveyed, then you might be in favor of wiping out the police review board as an unnecessary infringement on the police doing their job. But if you honestly believed that equal justice was a major problem, as do 65% of blacks surveyed, then you might see such a review board as an important level of protection.

If you truly cared about easing the tensions among the races in our community, you might want to test out whose perceptions are closer to the facts and do that in relationship with a person of the other race.

Perception can become a self-fulfilling prophesy. About half the blacks & whites in the survey believe they are disliked by members of the other race.

The study also revealed how far attitudes have changed in this country that 69% whites and 75% blacks favor full integration. But even if you personally are in favor of that, if you don't think your neighbor or business partner believes that, you may hesitate to raise the issue.

The survey indicated that a majority of whites 53% and 74% of blacks believe that "Most white people" either want to keep blacks down or don't care if they get ahead."

It was interesting that both races agree on what the big problems are that face NC. The top four problems which the majority of both races say we should focus on are:

1. Crime and violence
2. Economy, jobs, & unemployment
3. Drugs & Alcohol
4. Education and public schools

Now if both races agree that those are the major problems facing us, why is it we are not doing a better job of working together in solving these problems which we all see would be to our mutual benefits.

A major issue is our vastly differing perceptions surrounding these problems.Take jobs, for example. Do you think that blacks in NC have as good or better chance of getting a job that they are qualified for as white people? 69% of whites think they have as good or better a chance while 75% of blacks think they don't have as good a chance. That is almost a mirror image of each other in perception and your perception is what you act on.

Look at housing. Do you think African-Americans have as good a chance to buy a house that they can afford as does a white person? 81% of whites think that African-Americans have as good or better chance as whites to get what they can afford while 54% of blacks, more than a majority, don't think they have as good a chance despite the laws against discrimination.

Look at education. You have a son or daughter and you fill them with your hopes and dreams of improving themselves through education. You want to believe that education is dependent on a combination of ability and hard work.

89% of whites think blacks have as good or better chance to get a good education as do white people. 54% of blacks, a majority, think that is true but 38% of blacks, or over a third, don't believe it's true.

If you wanted to do one thing for race relations in NC, you would find out whose perceptions are closer to the truth. If the system is in fact stacked against people of one race, then making the system fair is most important thing that can be done. If the system is fair, then to help people who think it is unfair to change their perceptions will ease the tensions that exist in the state.

The interesting thing is that not only do 73% of whites but also 63% of blacks believe that if blacks tried harder, they could be as well off as whites. In fact, in contrast to those who think that blacks prefer preferential treatment, 51% of blacks opposed preferential treatment. In the focus groups, the majority of blacks said that they knew that they would have to work harder than whites to achieve the same end but they preferred to earn their own way.

With these huge gaps in perception of reality, it is clear that if we want better relationships between the races in North Carolina, we are going to have to close the gaps. In the survey, it was clear that the less contact a person had with members of the opposite race, the more negative was their perception & opinions of the other race. 62% whites and 76% of blacks say they find it hard to talk honestly about race with members of the other race, so we clearly need such conversations if we are to do anything but dwell in our misperceptions.

75% of whites and 93% of blacks say they want to get involved in improving relationships but their apprehensions about doing anything about it is probably reflected in the fact that only 11 % of whites and 16% of blacks wanted to increase their already limited contact with members of the opposite race.

If you want to improve race relations, the first thing you need to do is be willing to enter into a relationship with a person of another race in a manner that allows you to explore your own perceptions of reality. Where there is unfairness, it needs to be opposed and if it seems to you to be just a product of another person's imagination, then you need to be willing to enter into an investigation to see which perception is right.

WORSHIP

CHAPTER 4

A core element around which the discussion revolved in that initial lunch among three clergy, and the unifying feature that connected those who gathered in the original study group that gave birth to the Presbyterian Interracial Dialogue was the faith that is shaped by the Presbyterian heritage. As the Shorter Catechism of the Westminster Confession stated, the chief purpose of the lives of believers was "to glorify God and enjoy him forever." Therefore, it was natural as the Dialogue developed, to direct its attention to worship as one of the central elements of their faith.

As they continued to grow in their understanding of the complexity of racism, and as they interacted with others who were seeking to combat racism across the country, they became aware of how those who led anti-racism seminars made a distinction between prejudice and racism. Consider your own use of those terms. Do you use them interchangeably or do they refer to different dimensions of the racial divisions we are exploring?

Those who had participated in anti-racism training as part of Leadership Winston-Salem brought to the Dialogue the following distinction. **Prejudice** is an opinion or judgment, usually unfavorable, based on deeply held feelings and anecdotal experiences but not shaped by facts. For example, some Caucasians believe that the presence of African American residents in their neighborhood lowers property values. Some African Americans believe that most Caucasians dislike them merely on the basis of their skin color.

Racism is defined as prejudice with power. It requires two factors: 1. An individual's thoughts, feelings, language, and behavior that are based on the assumption of the dominant racial group that another racial or ethnic group is inferior to one's own, and 2. The power the individual (as a member of the dominant group) has to discriminate against or benefit from a society structured to favor one race over another.

An excerpt from an article in 1996 by Peggy McIntosh on the unconscious privilege of being white suggests that as a white you can:

1. Arrange to be in the company of people of your race most of the time without hindering what you want to do.
2. Go shopping alone and be fairly confident that you will not be hassled by store personnel regardless of how you are dressed.
3. Be sure your children will be given curricular materials that will testify to the existence of their race.
4. Take a strong public position without feeling like you are putting your race on trial.
5. If a traffic cop pulls you over, you can be pretty sure that you haven't been singled out because of your race.
6. Easily buy posters, cards, picture books, dolls, toys, and children's magazines featuring people of your own race.
7. Take a job with an affirmative action employer without coworkers suspecting that you got it because of your race.
8. Choose blemish cover or bandages in "flesh" color and have them more or less match your skin.

Most of us assume that to be racist is to be mean spirited or overtly bigoted. Maybe it also means just assuming the world is based on merit and unconsciously benefiting from the privilege of race.

The experience of worship, the Dialogue believed, had the capacity to transcend both prejudice and racism by inviting people to gather to give worth to that which was greater than all that divided them.

If you chose to draw upon the resources of worship to celebrate and affirm God's intention for how we relate in the diverse world that God created, how would you do it?

The first effort of the Dialogue was to make use of our heritage of hymns and music of faith. In January, 1994, a little over a year after the Dialogue began, the congregations were invited to a hymn sing at Highland Presbyterian Church. By this time, the Dialogue had grown to four churches, now including Trinity Presbyterian, and 150 people gathered for ice cream and to celebrate the music of our faith.

In that same year, 1994, the Dialogue began what was to become a yearly tradition of gathering for worship on the second Sunday in Advent. The first service was held on December 4 at Grace Presbyterian Church. The season of Advent celebrates Christ who came to reconcile the world to God's purpose and to affirm our calling as ambassadors of reconciliation and disciples of the Prince of Peace.

The call to worship of that first service was drawn from Isaiah 11:6, 9 spoken responsively.

Leader: I call upon the people of God to give voice to the promise of Isaiah.

People: The wolf shall live with the lamb, the leopard shall lie down with the kid, the calf and the lion and the fatling together, and a little child shall lead them.

Leader: I call upon the people of God to speak the vision of the peaceable kingdom.

People: They will not hurt or destroy on all my holy mountain; for the earth will be full of the knowledge of the Lord as the waters cover the sea.

With that stirring call, the service proceeded with Advent Scriptures and the music of the faith. Charles Burns from Dellabrook, Vaughn Thomas of Parkway, and Louise Foy from Grace Presbyterian guided the congregation musically while various members of the churches, lay and ordained, read the Scriptures. Dan Wilkers, the new pastor at Parkway, proclaimed the word.

The cover for the bulletin for this service carried the newly adopted mission statement of the Dialogue.

It is the mission of the Presbyterian Inter-Racial Dialogue, bonded by Christian love and caring . . .

- To begin to break down barriers which stand between us as black people and white people.
- To share knowledge and experiences which will enable us to know and understand one another.
- To become an active, viable witness of Christian love in our community.

In that same year, the four churches, Dellabrook, Grace, Trinity, and Highland chose to have a pulpit exchange on Sunday, September 18, 1994. By the following year, the Dialogue had grown to six churches, three predominantly Caucasian and three predominantly African American. The Dialogue agreed to continue the pulpit exchange on a yearly basis but chose Reformation Sunday in late October as the day for the exchange. They believed that Reformation Sunday was symbolic of the need for our churches to always pay attention to what God is doing among us to reform our witness in the area of race relations in Winston-Salem.

In some cases, in addition to the pastors exchanging pulpits, churches also benefited from exchanging choirs and hearing from other talented lay people in the congregations. One particularly moving example was a poem by RaVonda Dalton-Rann of Dellabrook during that churches exchange with Highland on October 26, 1997.

You are invited to read the poem out loud and imagine that you are either a member of High Land or Della Brook on that day.

> What am I on a rainy day like this? When I am wet
> cold surrounded by dark dreary air that doesn't linger
> in soothing sustenance but lurks about like a shadow
> Who am I standing before you? What purpose does
> it bring for me to pour my being and you to honor it
> by listening if we speak different languages if we walk

with unsynchronized steps if we share items that others do not need or appreciate?

Who are you?

There is a river flowing through me, brothers and sisters and it wants desperately for me to hear your mountains watch your trees bow to the wind as it calls your name as it calls your name

High

Land

Didn't you know that the wind was God's breath? And He speaks in it in rhythms and half notes and three quarter time and iambic pentameter and it is imperative that we learn the timing of His song and understand His lyrics before we are ever able to sing

Listen

Listen

there is a universal tone to His language

He makes it easy to hear and understand Him

Who am I to think that I can come here and expect you to know me?

Who are you to think that you can invite me and I will feel instant comfort?

Will you ever understand why I prefer Nikki Giovanni to Lord Byron

Or would rather learn of Hannibal than Napoleon

Or Roberta Flack to Carly Simon

Or Cliff Huxtable to Ward Cleaver

Or

Will you ever know

Why I prefer my grandmother's cold remedy to Nyquil Why I count the rounds on wooly worms or check the coat on my dog to see how cold it really is or why I worry when the leaves fall too soon

I pray for an easier time when we can know each other's signs

There is an unsettling air about those of us who believe that we are so equal that we are not different

I pray for a time that our uniqueness will be our badges of honor and each one will respect one and see rainbow that crosses continents and slide upon the colors down to earth and joy in praise of Europe and Mother Africa

I wanna hear our messenger
sing your song
I wanna surround myself
in your spirit
and speak in tongues
that bring comfort to your soul
I want to rise about all its and isms
that separate us
I want to walk among your ancestors and have them recognize the God in me
I want to sit with you in Heaven
and call you brother and sister
and mean it
I wanna climb to High Land
and watch
the clouds
form shapes that look like you
Who am I to think that I can go to High Land with you?

And who are you to think that you can ever touch the rippling of Della Brook?

I am a part of that brook
and I can nourish your soul
and you are the Land that feeds me
Who are we?

We are all imprisoned in the castles of our skin* let your castle be built next to mine and let us build a higher land with many brooks rippling in truth in praise

in sorrow
in earnest
in honor
in pain
in joy
in purpose
Let us all walk in the rain together
and know that we are all getting wet
Let the moisture soften each pore of all our skins
for we are experiencing God's tears and God's cleansing
spirit
Amen

*line taken from poem by Nikki Giovanni

In 2001, the Dialogue chose to augment their worship offerings by also having a Lenten Vespers at which they would gather at the table together.

The call to worship for the first Lenten service was drawn from Isaiah 58.

Leader: Is not this the fast I choose: to loose the bonds of injustice;

People: To share your bread with the hungry;

Leader: To bring the homeless poor into your house;

People: When you see the naked to clothe them?

Leader: Then your light will break forth like the dawn,

People: And your healing shall spring up quickly.

Recognizing the importance of continually reaching beyond themselves, the offering from this first Lenten service was given in support of the new Hispanic ministry that was being established by Salem Presbytery.

As the Dialogue continued to explore ways to build the beloved community, they were conscious of the generational divisions that also needed to be bridged. A particularly significant decision was to involve the youth from the congregations as participants in the Advent services

– both in choirs and in reading Scriptures. Youth and adults, male and female, black and white gave voice to praise the God who united them.

These special worship experiences and the work of the Dialogue drew the attention of the larger church. On two occasions, this resulted in the moderator of the national church coming to proclaim the word during our services.

In 1997, Pat Brown preached at our Advent service at Parkway Presbyterian. She accepted the invitation even though it took place on her birthday. During the service, she explained her decision by saying that over thirty years ago she was in a Greensboro jail for having demonstrated against segregation and now stood before an inter-racially packed church of people committed to combating racism. Sam Stevenson was a student at North Carolina A&T University at the same time and had participated in the same events.

During the Lenten service in 2004, the Dialogue welcomed Susan Andrews, the moderator of the national church for that year. In addition to being moderator of the church, she was also the pastor at Bradley Hills Presbyterian in Bethesda, Maryland where Steve McCutchan had served as an associate in the early '70s.

One particular worship experience demonstrated both the commitment to and the occasional discomfort of learning to be honest with each other in making our witness. Early in the Dialogue's practice of having a pulpit exchange, one pastor chose to be boldly honest and intentionally confrontive in proclaiming the word for his first time at Highland. Some of the comments by elders at Highland reflect the diversity within that church and the Dialogue.

"Carlton seems to echo what I've heard others say."

"I question the use of the pulpit to express his personal agenda."

"His Christian perspective is more poignant than ours."

"I don't care to be preached at."

"He awakened me from my complacency and comfort."

"He got our attention and that is important."

"He's very smart but at times he has the demeanor of arrogance."

"It wasn't until the Dialogue that I realized how racist I was."

"He seems to refuse to look at individuals but makes group judgments."

"I see Carlton playing the role of a prophet and that is confrontive."

"I think he went too far for a first sermon."

The exchanges continued and enriched the churches but also made a witness to the community. As John Railey, religious columnist for the Winston-Salem Journal in 2002, said in an article about the pulpit exchange that year,

"In these days when black congregations and white ones often share worship, there's a strong emphasis on being colorblind, on trying to lose our Southern obsession with race. . . Yet regardless of what some of us might insist, we're not colorblind and never will be. We're only a high profile murder or police beating case away from our next national shouting match between blacks and whites. We often yell about race instead of talk about race and all the hang-ups we still have about it.

"Which is what Eversley's appearance at Parkway was all about. 'The communication (between the races) is often times garbled,' he said. He spoke as part of the 10-year anniversary of the Presbyterian Interracial Dialogue, a group of black churches and white ones that talk and act. . .This group went beyond self-consciousness about race.

"It went beyond a few moments of feeling warm and fuzzy together.

"It became the largest and best-organized interracial group of churches in the country. But most important, it acted."

Worship has continued to be at the center of the Dialogue whether it is during the high holy days of Advent and Lent or at the dedication of a Habitat House for a new resident. Frequently it is accompanied by food and always the gathering of good friends. Sometimes it is specifically Christian worship and sometimes it is an inclusive worship that recognizes and respects the distinctive traditions of Christians, Jews, and Muslims. Always it is a reminder that we are accountable to a God that transcends our divisions and heals of us of our wounds without blurring the distinctions that mark our diversity.

As one of the Dialogue newsletters stated, what we are about is expressed in Einstein's theory of relativity, $E=MC^2$ or equality equals mutual care squared.

FROM GENERATION TO GENERATION

CHAPTER 5

What do you think? Are hate and prejudice genetic? If not, what are the factors that contribute towards people developing prejudice attitudes? Do you agree with that simple song from the movie, *South Pacific*?:

You've got to be taught to hate – that it is not natural.

Is it true that hate and fear have to be drummed into you – to be afraid of people oddly made or of a different shade?

Is it true, as the song suggests, that our prejudices are taught to mimic all the people our relatives hate?

As the Dialogue grew in their understanding of the complexity of racism in the society, they recognized that it was not enough to educate themselves. They also had to reach out and engage others in the conversation about racism. If you were in a similar study group and you wanted to reach out in a positive manner to those with whom you were in regular contact, where would you begin?

Remember that from the beginning, the group wanted to draw upon the resources and opportunities that were a natural part of their being people of faith in Presbyterian churches. While it is easy for cynics to point to the failings of the church in the area of race, it is also historically true in both the black and white communities that the church has also been the arena in which people have explored how to improve race relations.

In the fall of 1995, members of the dialogue became aware of a racially negative experience by Amanda Bethea, one of the youth at Grace. It happened at a Synod youth gathering. It alerted the Dialogue that there were very few settings where youth can explore their own experiences affected by race. The Dialogue began to explore how they might provide an opportunity for a youth dialogue. While they wanted to share the positive benefits of the Dialogue with more people, they felt a special responsibility for the youth of their churches.

On March 16, 1996, two youth leaders from each church came to a planning meeting at Grace under the leadership of Maggie Henderson, associate pastor at Highland, and Carlton Eversley from Dellabrook. Together they explored the types of experiences that youth were having in their schools, church, and work. The youth were eager for the opportunity to process their individual experiences and to shape a positive response to the racial tensions in their society. Each agreed to discuss the possibility of creating a youth dialogue with the peers of their churches and to bring their ideas to a meeting on July 11 at Highland.

At this second meeting, they decided to have a picnic on September 14, 1996 for interested young people in their churches. All middle school and high school youth from the six churches were invited. After a couple of similar get-acquainted meetings, the youth chose to work together on behalf of others. They held their December 21 meeting at Amos cottage where they provided a party for the developmentally disabled children who lived there. Then on Saturday, January 11, they met together for a tour of Winston-Salem with the purpose of breaking down the stereotypes that they might have of different sections in Winston-Salem.

They recognized that youth, like adults, tend to live in selected parts of a city and only have impressions of other parts. These impressions are often based on false information that make people reluctant to visit those areas. They wanted, through their tour, to break down their stereotypes and appreciate the larger diversity in Winston-Salem.

Though it began strong, lack of consistent adult leadership caused the youth dialogue to flounder for the last half of 1997. Then, in January of 1998, the meetings revived when the youth at Grace invited the Dialogue youth to meet and hear about their pastor, Sam Stevenson's recent trip to Ethiopia. At that meeting, the Grace youth challenged the other Dialogue churches to reciprocate. Norman Brown, an elder at Lloyd, met with the youth to do more planning, and on March 8, the Highland youth accepted Grace's challenge and invited the Dialogue youth to a Pizza and Bowling Party.

The rather erratic efforts at forming a continuing youth dialogue took a significant step forward in March 1999. This change was the culmination of a conversation that had been taking place for almost 7 years.

As part of the Dialogue's efforts to support the revitalization of ministry at Lloyd, the Dialogue had been in conversation with presbytery about support for a position that would provide a part-time pastor for Lloyd and also a part-time position on presbytery staff to assist the several African American churches in the presbytery. These discussions began shortly after the Dialogue was formed in 1992. In March of that year, the Dialogue created a position paper advocating for the presbytery part of that partnership. It said in part, "This person would be an enabler for the (Black) Caucus/congregational purpose of achieving the full participation of racial/ethnics in church and society, focusing on concerns stemming from racial/ethnic religious, cultural, and political tradition and speaking to those issues which affects most directly the lives of racial/ethnic people."

This led to conversations with Mike Warren, Associate Presbyter of Salem Presbytery and Willie Garvin, financial administrator of the presbytery to seek sources of funding that might support a half-time pastor at Lloyd and a half-time Racial Justice Advocate. A new job description was prepared and a funding plan was created seeking help from the Small Church Task Force of presbytery, grants from synod and the General Assembly of the Presbyterian Church, and contribution from Dialogue churches.

Parallel to these efforts, Grace Presbyterian began to explore the option of placing an educator on their staff. By 1998, they had begun a four-year plan of setting aside some funds towards this possibility. Two years into this plan a series of events occurred that at first seemed unrelated but fit together in a way that makes Presbyterians smile at the evidence of the providential hand of God. First, there was the collapse of the Project Freedom ministry of six churches in another part of the presbytery. Willie Garvin of the presbytery staff alerted Sam Stevenson to the fact that Clarisse Durnell, a recently employed educator for that project was going to be laid off. As Sam talked to Steve McCutchan at one of their bi-monthly breakfasts about Grace's interest in employing an educator, the idea of combining Grace's interests with that of the Dialogue began to form. In addition, Ms. Garvin, who had been part of the earlier discussions about seeking funds for Lloyd, pointed out that there was still 8 months of grant money remaining from the Project Freedom approved ministry.

While Presbyterians would never suggest that one ministry would collapse to provide resources for another ministry, they did believe that God was not defeated by negative circumstances, and that perhaps this could be an example of God enabling new life to emerge from negative reality. Building on the previous job descriptions, a new proposal was quickly formed to present to both the Dialogue and Grace. The idea was for Grace to fund half of the position, the other Dialogue churches to fund the other half of the position but with about eight months of grant money to provide them time to secure such commitments.

This was be the first time that the separate congregations were asked to provide financial support for the ministry of the Dialogue. For 1999, they also had about $10,000 remaining from the Project Freedom Grant. Grace agreed to provide almost $17,000 for the half-time position of educator. Highland and Parkway were asked to provide $4,000 each, Trinity was asked for $1,000 and Dellabrook and Lloyd were asked to provide $900 and $500 respectively.

Clarisse began as a Volunteer in Mission for Education at Grace (half- time) and Dellabrook one-fourth time and one-fourth time with Lloyd and PIRD. At Grace, her responsibilities included youth and children, teaching the second Sunday in their church school, and general support for and training of the teachers. At Dellabrook, her focus was to be on the youth, including providing a Bible study after worship on the first Sunday. At Lloyd, she had particular responsibility for the Helping Hands tutoring program for neighborhood children on Mondays and to provide a children's sermon on the Third Sunday. In addition, she was to help coordinate an inter-racial dialogue for the youth of the six churches.

You can easily see what a complex job description this was. The clergy of the Dialogue rented a truck and supplied willing hands to help Clarisse move from her previous location in Salisbury to her new home in Winston-Salem. Clarisse proved to be capable of maneuvering through this quagmire of multiple employers. She had a major impact on the development of a stable interracial youth dialogue. For almost three and one-half years, Clarisse provided the energy and imagination needed to demonstrate the value of an inter-racial youth dialogue. It was also the beginning of the six churches becoming financially committed to the support of the Dialogue work. Eventually, in 2001, they would take the next step and form a council with formal by-laws and institutional stability for the ministry that until that time was guided by the clergy.

Under Clarisse's guidance, the youth dialogue took on new life. The first major event was a sleepover at Grace. Here was an extended time for forty youth of the six churches to enjoy food, fun, and a deepening of their relationships. A particularly poignant part of the discussion was around the recent events at the Columbine High School in Colorado. Dan Wilkers guided this discussion as well as using his skill with the guitar to help the youth process their response to this recent event in which many young people their age were either killed or injured.

Clarisse quickly formed a youth council to meet quarterly to plan the future events. One of the first events following the sleepover was a scavenger hunt held in a nearby shopping mall, using Polaroid cameras. After the scavenger hunt was complete, the youth returned to Trinity. In addition to sharing pizza, they began to organize a shoebox project that was to deliver school supplies to impoverished schools in Eastern North Carolina.

In January 2000, Salem Presbytery held a meeting with the Dialogue clergy celebrating Clarisse's first year with the Dialogue churches and securing financial commitments from the six churches and presbytery to renew her contract for another year. On March 5, 2000, the Dialogue celebrated her first year and held a formal installation service that recognized her excellent work.

With Clarisse's support, the youth council began to plan regular events that mixed fun and service. In March 2,000 there was a Tye-Dye Party followed by another sleepover in May. In the fall, the Dialogue youth planted trees and built a bench at the new playground at Lloyd.

Like the adult Dialogue, the youth discovered that their relationships grew as they engaged in fellowship, discussion, food, worship, and service. Like a rubber band pulled between two fingers, when they reached out to someone beyond them, they were pulled closer together.

As 2001 began, the youth outreach continued. In February, they met at the Winston-Salem Rehabilitation Health Care Center to share with the elderly residents in singing and bingo with prizes the youth provided. They also began selling T-shirts as a means of funding some of their future activities. Then in May, the youth responded to having learned that Clarisse had been diagnosed with Retinitis Pigmentosa by organizing a Rock-a-thon. They met at Parkway and rocked in rocking chairs from 9 p.m. until 9 a.m. with a goal of raising $2,000 for the Fighting Blindness Foundation.

In July 2001, some of the Dialogue youth attended a youth conference at Winston-Salem State organized by Clarisse and Carlton. Clarisse also took some youth to the Youth Triennium at Purdue University.

In 2002, the youth crossed the bridges between faiths and reached out to the youth of Temple Emanuel and the Masjid Al-Mu-minun to organize a Café night to raise funds for the second Habitat build. This event symbolized much of the purpose of the Dialogue. Youth from across both racial and religious communities gathered with an interracial and interfaith community of adults to reach beyond all of them to provide a home for a family, Mia Anthony and her son, Ojie, who had become members of Grace Presbyterian. As Mia expressed it to the Dialogue, "Words cannot express the gratitude that I feel for all you have done for my son and me. I thank God for this occasion, and I thank God for you. . .Each day in our new home will be a reminder to my son and me of the debt we owe to others because of what you have done for us."

After three years of helping the Dialogue fulfill their dream of a consistent youth dialogue, Clarisse received a call to become the educator of a Presbyterian church in Dover, Delaware and finished her work with the Dialogue churches on July 31, 2002. During her three years, she had created a youth council and recruited some committed adults to work with the council. The Dialogue counsel began the deliberation of what to do next.

By the following summer, the Dialogue had hired Angela V. Gerena-Diaz, a member at Dellabrook, as a part time youth worker to help guide the youth dialogue. Following the pattern formed by Clarisse, Angela worked with a youth council to develop both fun experiences and service projects in the community. One new type of event was in connection with the Wake Forest Divinity to help youth consider a theological vocation and how they relate spirituality to their lives. In addition, they continued to have a mixture of fun and service activities

When the Dialogue chose to build a third Habitat house in 2006, the youth again brought their creativity to play in raising money for the build. This time in addition to their talent night, they held a silent auction for their services. The youth would pair up and offer such work as lawn mowing, mulch spreading, baby-sitting, cooking dinner, etc.

While the most consistent part of the youth dialogue was during the time with Clarisse Durnell, over the twenty years of the Dialogue there has been a variety of ways that the churches drew upon the interests and creativity of their youth to provide an example of interracial, interfaith community. In many ways, the Dialogue experienced what society has begun to recognize, that the separation of races and faith is less an issue for them. They were far more comfortable than the adults in enjoying each other and appreciating their differences while not being set a part by them.

An example of what we have to learn from our youth is seen in an essay by one of the youth participants, Michael Spangler, son of Laura and Tom Spangler. It is of particular interest to the Dialogue because of their continuing interest in issues surrounding public education in our community. In 2003, he won a contest with the following essay:

Here in Winston-Salem, there is a large amount of cultural diversity, especially in the downtown area. There you can see the beauty of different cultures and races coming together. I, a white, male teenager, am a member of a small, predominantly African-American church downtown, Lloyd Presbyterian, and it is good to see faces of many colors and ages gather there peacefully. However, in Winston-Salem, there is a big problem with race that many people don't realize – resegregation in schools.

Our schools have been on the road toward resegregation since 1994, when the Winston-Salem Forsyth County school system was redistricted. Ironically, one goal of this plan was to racially integrate schools. To make sure this goal was attained, the WS/FCS Board of Education formed the Equity Committee to provide an annual report on equity issues of the new plan. The Committee's last report was in 2001, and since then it has been officially disbanded. Excerpts from their yearly reports include:

"Schools are becoming more racially and economically segregated" (1997).

"Increasing lack of racial and socioeconomic diversity of schools in the redistricted zones"(1998).

"Negative perceptions regarding Equity+ (schools with 75% or more of their students on free or reduced lunch) and minority race schools" (1999).

"Our continuing concern with the lack of racial and economic diversity of too many of our schools" (2000).

"Inequities in human and financial support." (2001).

Additionally, ten elementary schools in our district are Equity+, and all ten of those schools, as well as the two Equity+ middle schools, have a student body that is over 90% minority. Today the high school I attend, which is not Equity+, remains the most segregated , with 77.8% of our student body being white.

However harmonious race relations may seem in Winston-Salem, today there is almost no difference between a poor school and a minority school. These bitter inequities were only made worse by the disbanding of the Equity Committee, so that now racial inequality in our schools will worsen unless something is done.

I was there on the night that the Committee's fate was decided, and Geneva Brown, the only African-American woman on the Board, was the one vote out of twelve to keep the Equity Committee. After the meeting, the group in attendance congregated in the auditorium of Central Office and talked about what the decision meant for the community.

Everyone was in agreement that it is vital for children to be exposed to diversity in school. When a child is in a school where everyone is the same color, he or she may grow up thinking that is the way the world is. If children and young adults are not exposed to diversity in school, then they will not be prepared for the real world, and we have not accomplished much in our goal of racial harmony.

I believe that there is hope for the children of Winston-Salem. Everyone should be informed of what is going on and should be aware of the great importance of ethnic diversity for our schools. We need new leadership in the Board of Education people who care more about children than the budget crunch. Most importantly the people of Winston-Salem need to care more about the equity issues of our schools if we want our city to be a place of racial and cultural harmony."

As you can see, the benefit of the Dialogue's work with the youth not only benefited the youth but the adults and the larger community.

THE LARGER COMMUNITY

CHAPTER 6

I f you study the impact and complexity of racism in your life and community, how do you think it will affect the way that you read the newspaper, hear about things that are happening in your community, and enter into conversation with your neighbors? From the initial lunch of the three pastors, it was always their understanding that while they began with studying and conversation, it would, at the appropriate time, lead to some type of action. Racism doesn't just affect your personal psyches. It also tears at the bonds of the community. The challenge of racism can't be resolved just by education. It also requires changes in structures of the community. For Presbyterians, the community of the church is only part of the larger community in which they are engaged.

Community structures are intended to bring order into a society and most member of a community prefer to leave the decisions about the structure to those elected or hired to maintain that order while the rest of the populace focuses on the daily challenges and pleasures of their lives. However, when you have been studying both the history and the current impact of racism on your society, you tend to raise a new set of questions about those structures. What are some of the questions that you think you would raise out of such an experience?

The issues of justice from the national response to the Rodney King trial to the local issues of the murder of a hobo, the death of an incarcerated woman, and the death of a policeman because of the actions of some teenagers led to that initial lunch. It is perhaps fitting that it was an issue of justice that first invited the Dialogue to enter the arena of advocacy.

To understand how this issue was especially sensitive to a diverse group studying racism together, it is helpful to jump ahead a few years and see some results reported in a United Way Study of race in our community. Partly because of the tensions in 1992, the United Way of Winston-Salem had commissioned a study of the impact of race on our community to follow up on a larger study done on racial attitudes in North Carolina. Carlton Eversley and Stephen McCutchan were part of the United Way Task Force that was formed in 1996 (to choose how to respond to the report that was released in February 1997.)

While the members of the Dialogue had been wrestling with understanding how being black or white altered one's view of what was taking place in our society, the report was able to measure the differing perspectives of our larger community. One of their findings was that black citizens and white citizens had almost mirror images of how they viewed the legal system.

When asked, "Do you think the law enforcement officers in our community are generally tougher on whites than blacks, tougher on blacks than whites, or do the officers treat them both the same?" 65% of White people said they were treated the same and 64% of Black people believed they were tougher on blacks. When asked, "Do blacks generally get equal justice in North Carolina or is getting equal justice a major problem for blacks in the state?", 60% of white people said blacks generally get justice while 65% of black people said justice is a major problem

While most white citizens assume that the police and courts exist to protect them from criminals and other miscreants, that is not true among a large proportion of black citizens. Imagine what it means to live in a society where you sincerely believe that the legal system is stacked against you. Too many black citizens can tell a personally painful experiences or know friends and relatives who have had experiences of either the police or the courts working against them. While a white citizen might feel a sense of security to see a uniformed officer present, many black citizens view the presence of the same uniformed officer with mixed emotions.

As white members of the Dialogue learned, this conflicted view of the justice system is exacerbated for black parents of teenagers. As one African American pastor told Steve McCutchan, "The day that my son got his driver's license, my fear level went up. Not only did I need to worry about the normal challenges of teenagers getting in trouble, but as an African American parent, I also had to worry that a black teenager with an attitude might trigger an uptight police officer and result in my son being shot."

Steve McCutchan was participating in a "ride along" program with a police officer when he experienced a fortunately mild version of what the pastor was referring to. The officer with which he was riding stopped to chat with another officer on foot patrol. While they were talking, some African American teens rode by on their bicycles. The foot patrol officer made some racist remarks about the teens and how he would make sure they didn't cause any trouble. While it was "tough talk" designed to impress, and while it was probably the result of the officer's experience of having to deal with numerous incidents involving teenagers, the "profiling" of the African American teenagers was a reminder of the concern of the African American parent.

With that background, you can now understand the Dialogue's involvement in a community issue around the Police Review Board. In 1993, the Board of Alderman had voted to establish a police review board as a three-year experiment. It was an appeal process to respond when anyone believed that they were being treated unfairly. It was staffed by volunteers and had resolved several complaints without conflict. After its first year of operation, the Police Chief stated that he did not believe that it was causing a morale problem in his department. In April 1, 1994, after one year of the three year trial, the Board of Alderman thought that it was both controversial and unnecessary. White members of the Dialogue understood why the black members of the Dialogue and therefore black citizens in general, viewed such a decision with suspicion.

It seemed that this might be an appropriate time to act in a way that put into action some of their newly acquired awareness of the complexity of race in their community. The clergy of the Dialogue arranged a meeting with Mayor Martha Wood to express their concern. They also chose to speak on behalf of the Police Review Board to the May 1994 meeting of the Board of Alderman.

Elder Betty Jones from Highland and Reverend Stevenson made a presentation to the Board of Alderman on behalf of the Dialogue. Among their remarks, they said,

"As members of the Presbyterian Interracial Dialogue, we have discussed the impact that perceptions have on our relationships with one another. We see the positive impact which the Police Review Board has on our city as it offers an objective hearing ground for both citizens and the police. As a result, it increases both the perceptions and the reality of justice and fairness for everyone in our city.

We urge you in your deliberations to follow a course of action which will contribute to the health of our city. Frankly, too often we observe actions in government that are divisive and adversarial. We hope that will not be the situation here – there is too much at stake."

Eventually the Aldermen chose to continue the Police Review Board and it continues to this day. Did the Dialogue's presentation make a difference? Whether it did or not, there was satisfaction in having spoken up for what they believed. Another finding from the study of racism in North Carolina was that the majority of blacks did not believe that most whites cared about how blacks felt. At least in this case, the white members of the Dialogue knew that their black friends in the Dialogue knew that they cared.

Another continuing concern that attracted the attention of the Dialogue was what was happening with respect to public education in Winston-Salem. In response to some pressures towards eliminating busing and restoring neighborhood schools in 1994, the Board of Education was considering redistricting in a manner that raised the question of whether the system was moving towards the resegregation of our public education in Winston-Salem.

While the school system was moving in this direction, Dr. Martin, Superintendent of the Winston-Salem/Forsyth County schools, was aware that attention needed to be paid to the failure of their curriculum to be sufficiently sensitive to the diverse nature of our country. As part of their response, the school system contracted with Dr. Alton Pollard of Wake Forest University, to design a method to augment the curriculum and address the need to educate the students to the role played by various minorities in the history of our country. In 1993, Dr. Pollard was invited to address the Dialogue on this development.

This became known as the *Infusion Project* and Carlton Eversley and Steve McCutchan were invited to be part of the development of this project. So, on the one hand, members of the Dialogue were involved in improving the school curriculum but also they were raising concerns about changes in policy and structure that they believed harmed the students. (Michael Spangler's essay in Chapter 5 describes these concerns.)

As part of the Dialogue's exploration of the subject, in March of 1995, members were invited to view a documentary about what had happened in the Charlotte education system. One pleasant surprise was discovering that one of the participants in the Dialogue, Ellen Doyle, had been involved in some of the discussions in Charlotte and was one of the people interviewed in the film.

In April of 1995, a delegation from the Dialogue met with Dr. Martin, to share their concern for the direction that the Board of Education was moving, which they believed would lead to greater segregation in the schools and the impoverishment of all the students.

Later, in 1998, when the Board of Education threatened to defund the *Infusion Project* that they had created, members of the Dialogue were among those who came to its defense and helped maintain the project. In preparation for Elder Fred Terry and Pastor Laura Spangler speaking to the Board of Education, a letter was sent to the Board. In that letter and the later presentation, the Dialogue expressed their concern with proposals to weaken the infusion project by eliminating the position of coordinator for the project. In part, they said:

While the success of that project has been slow, we have been quite pleased with its success in the schools where it has been fully implemented.. . .

Dr. Martin has stated his support for the continuing use of this curriculum but has also proposed eliminating the coordinator position and assigning its task as part of a position already burdened with several other responsibilities. We question the wisdom of removing this crucial component while the project is at such a crucial stage. Absent of central administrative oversight and someone who is willing to work at overcoming the resistance which has already surfaced, we fear that the program is being consigned to failure.

In light of the current question of whether the schools will be able to successfully be integrated under the current plan, we find it even more crucial that all of our students receive an education which will inform them of the rich strength of our diverse culture. Without such an education we fear that we may be contributing to the perpetuation of the racial attitudes which have resulted in many of our current social divisions. We would urge you to reconsider the elimination of the position of coordinator and to re-examine the means by which the administration might make even a stronger demonstration of its support for this critical program.

We were very surprised to hear that a major component of that program, the position of coordinator, is being eliminated before the program has even been fully developed. As you are aware, even the first stage of the project has yet to be introduced into all the schools. Site evaluation at the schools which have accepted the program suggests that a number of teachers have yet to fully accept the importance of the program. The original vision of the program was to introduce it into the social studies area with the African-American component. Following the success of that aspect, it was to be further developed in two directions. Other areas of curriculum such as English, science, math, etc. were to be developed in a similar manner. Also other racial and ethnic groups were to have their culture added to the process. In our community it would be particularly important that this take place with respect to Hispanic and Asian contributions to our lives.

The Community Advisory Group, which gave so much of their time in developing this curriculum, believed we were contributing to the initial stages of providing a more complete education for all of our children who will have to live in an increasingly pluralistic world. It was our conviction that all of our children were being cheated of a quality education which would prepare them for our society.

The concern for our public education system has continued to be a concern of the Dialogue for twenty years. They have tried to raise awareness about policy problems and be engaged in various direct actions to assist the schools. Among other actions, Grace Presbyterian became involved in a hall monitoring program at Carver and a mentoring program at Ibraham elementary school. Several of their men both served as hall monitors at the high school and worked with children at the elementary school.

In addition to becoming involved in select issues within the Winston-Salem community, the Dialogue was aware of and sensitive to how racism was reflected in our churches. In May 1995, the Dialogue was invited to offer a workshop at the Pathways education event of our presbytery on the work of the Dialogue and how other churches could create their own Dialogue.

An incident occurred at the October 12-14, 1995 meeting of the Synod of the Mid-Atlantic that illuminated the benign but no less painful form of institutional racism that exists in our church structures.

Some background is helpful. In 1992, in response to budgetary challenges, the synod began to examine possible reorganization which would include staff reductions, including the Associate for Campus ministry and support staff. The plan was presented at the 1994 Synod meeting and rejected after some heated discussion and some polarization around these actions surfaced. The Reverend Carol Jenkins, synod executive, and Joseph Pickard who had been rehired as Associate Executive for Finance, were asked to continue to work on a new plan.

By December of 1994, the trustees of the synod had received some anonymous allegations charging Dr. Jenkins, who was African American, of mismanagement and incompetence. In 1995, the trustees formed a three-member task force to meet with the executive to address the complaints. There were 18 allegations, 15 of which were financially related and three related to personnel issues. The comptroller of the Synod examined the financial allegations and concluded that with one minor exception, they were related to internal policies and did not violate generally accepted auditing standards.

Those who were unhappy with these conclusions tried to take the accusations to the public media and also sent a letter to each of the presbytery executives in the Synod. The Richmond Times-Dispatch proceeded to take the allegations at face value and wrote an article critical of Dr. Jenkins. The Synod Council received the results of the investigation in 1995 exonerating Dr. Jenkins of any wrongdoing but the Trustees asked that an independent committee of five be appointed to review the financial and management practices of the Synod office.

When the synod next met, many felt the tone of the debate and the decisions of the trustees were reflections of racist attitudes and the African American commissioners along with several Caucasian supporters chose to walk out of the Synod meeting.

One of the commissioners, the Reverend James Mitchum, supported by the Dialogue, petitioned the Salem Presbytery Council to take two actions in response to the incident. First, to urge the synod to dissolve the "Committee of Five" and accept the report of the Executive Committee exonerating Dr. Jenkins as the Synod's final response to the allegations made. Second, it requested that Salem Presbytery ask the synod council to take the initiative to provide a symposium in each presbytery to address the subject of racism. In support of their requests the Dialogue said, "We call upon the Synod of the Mid-Atlantic to take seriously the extent of the pain among our African American brothers and sisters reflected in this dramatic action and to seek opportunities for listening, reflecting, and learning together concerning the sometimes subtle, sometimes blatant menace of racism."

Acting on their own request, Salem Presbytery asked Dale Walker, moderator of the Peace Making Committee to arrange an opportunity for the commissioners of Salem Presbytery to have a conversation about racism.

If you were planning such a dialogue experience for Salem Presbytery, what questions do you think would be helpful for members of our churches to discuss together? Remember that it will be at most a two-hour experience. What might help people break down some of the barriers and hear each other's concerns? What would help black Presbyterians feel like their discomfort was being heard? What would help white Presbyterians understand the difference between the interracial church they believe in and the way in which it is experienced by many minority groups within our denomination?

The Dialogue, working with other members of Presbytery, designed a conversation. They began with a brief skit followed by ten different people making statements that illustrated the disparity and inequality of the races in the United States. They ranged from statements about the country to statements about Salem Presbytery. The final statement was, "More than once, Salem Presbytery has sent all white delegations into regional, statewide, national, or international arenas. More than once, Salem Presbytery has had worship services with all white leadership. From a black perspective, it is the former Yadkin Presbytery (a previously predominantly African American Presbytery that merged with other predominantly Caucasian Presbyteries in 1983) that makes Salem distinctive. Otherwise, Concord and Orange unite on a nearly all white to white level."

Following this ten-minute introduction, small groups were formed and led by trained leaders. People were asked to share some personal responses to the experience of racism in their own lives. Next, as a means of moving from talk to action, the people in each small group were presented with a "Covenant for Racial Justice" and asked to explain why they would or would not sign it and if they were willing to take it back to their sessions to sign. Then, as a final act, they were asked to identify two or three actions that Presbytery could take to combat racism in the Presbytery.

The Covenant for Racial Justice read as follows:

We, the session of _____ commit ourselves to the work of racial justice. To this end, we pledge:

- To pray regularly for the healing of racism within ourselves, our family, our church, our community, our country, and around the world.
- To recognize the presence of racism in our church and our society and have courage to confront it.
- To study and meditate upon the way of justice according to Jesus' teaching and apply this learning in our living.

- To become involved in the struggle against institutional racism by: a) joining at least one organization that is dedicated to racial justice; b) participating in an interracial group and seeking to understand the perspective of those who are different from us.
- To evaluate our progress within six months of this pledge.

If you had been in such a group, how do you think you would have responded? If you had taken it back to your church, how do you think they would have responded?

When we move from general discussion to personal action and ask for a specific response from a group with which we are involved, many of our insecurities emerge. If you examine the covenant closely, there are few things that people who care about healing the divisions of race would object to. Yet for many within the presbytery on the day of discussion, defenses were raised and resistance to making a commitment to which they could be held accountable emerged. For many Presbyterian African Americans, it confirmed the entrenchment of racism even within our churches.

For the Dialogue it was a strong reminder that the infection of racism was not restricted to people of evil intent but infuses the lives of well-intentioned people and is intermeshed with fears and anxieties that are not easily addressed. For members of the presbytery, it was the planting of seeds, the growth of which was not in the control of the Dialogue.

In late 1997, another issue arose within Winston-Salem that exacerbated the racial suspicions within our community. In November the city elected a new mayor, Jack Cavanaugh. Later it was discovered that Mr. Cavanaugh had been present at a meeting of a group associated with the Ku Klux Klan and during that meeting had participated in saluting the Confederate Flag. Because the Dialogue had already created a framework for inter-racial discussions around such issues, it was decided that this was an opportunity to clarify what had happened.

Sam Stevenson and Steve McCutchan were asked to make an appointment with the Mayor and invite him to address the Dialogue at a future meeting. The intention of the meeting was not to be confrontive but to offer the mayor a public forum at which he could respond to the concerns about his behavior. Stevenson and McCutchan extended the invitation and discussed with the mayor possible ways to approach the subject.

Because of the publicity surrounding the mayor's actions, the meeting held at Highland Presbyterian in January of 1998 was one of the largest meetings that the Dialogue had held. While Mayor Cavanaugh seemed unable to comprehend the implications of his actions or an effective way to address them in this interracial setting, it did demonstrate the importance of the relationships that had been created by the Dialogue.

Later, in 2007, when Salem Presbytery was moving through a transition of staff, the members of the Dialogue became concerned that the presbytery was insufficiently sensitive to the importance of building a diverse staff at the presbytery level. A letter was formed from the Dialogue raising this issue for the people in charge of calling a new presbytery staff – interestingly the temporary head of that staff was Steve McCutchan, formerly of the Dialogue. McCutchan made use of that letter to reinforce his own efforts in that direction. The presbytery was able to construct one of the most diverse staffs within the denomination.

In 2010 tragedy in Haiti struck. The Dialogue had a personal connection with this country because one of its member churches, Parkway Presbyterian, had developed extensive mission work in Haiti. The Dialogue responded by both financial gifts and support of a medical relief trip. Dr. Tom Spangler, husband of pastor Laura Spangler, led a medical relief trip and later Parkway spearheaded an additional trip that involved other members of the Dialogue churches.

During the entire twenty years of the Dialogue's existence, in addition to addressing the concerns within the church community, they have continued to be responsive to the needs of the larger community, both nationally and internationally. They found the strength of their unity in diversity in both caring for each other and in caring for those in need beyond the boundaries of their churches. They were formed in response to the divisions caused by racial attitudes. They found strength in response to the vision of their Gospel that God loved the whole world.

RELATIONSHIPS BIRTH MINISTRIES

CHAPTER 7

As one member of the Dialogue said, "Maybe one of the reasons God created such a diverse world is that relating to those who are different from us prepares us to meet God who is totally different from any of us." We worship a God of hope and our journey unfolds in exciting and unexpected ways. As the Dialogue spent the past twenty years together, they have been continually surprised by the creativity and unexpected ways in which these relationships have given birth to new opportunities for ministry.

In the fall of 1998, Jane Goco, a newer participant in the Dialogue, proposed a new ministry expanding the community in which the Dialogue was involved. Inspired by the example of Jesus who sent his disciples out two by two, she proposed that teams of two, one white and one black, be formed to visit residents of local nursing homes that normally do not receive many visitors. In doing so, she suggested, we fulfill two tenets of the Dialogue's mission statement. The team would grow in their knowledge of each other even as they became an active viable witness of Christian love in the community.

On November 11, 1998, the Presbyterian Inter-racial Dialogue's Nursing Home Visitation Project held an organizational luncheon meeting at the Winston-Salem Rehabilitation and Healthcare Center. Under Jane's leadership, Micki Mabry of Trinity, Flo Winfree of

Highland, Doris Lewis of Parkway, Bertha Roundtree and Ernestine Worley of Grace, and Inis Johnson of Dellabrook worked to form twelve interracial teams to initiate the visitations.

One year later, on November 19, 2000, twenty-five women gathered at Parkway to celebrate the first year of the project. Samori Johnson, the Activity Director at the Rehabilitation Center was present to report on the remarkable difference this has made in the lives of many nursing home residents. Two men volunteered to participate in the following year. Jane Goco also became a consultant to some Baptist church members who wanted to replicate the idea at the Bowman Gray School of Medicine's Sticht Center for Aging. By November of 2000, the project had inspired the Tocar project at the Sticht Center that was funded by the Duke Foundation as a model for others around the country.

Theodora Fowler augmented this ministry by inviting Dialogue members to join Grace's quilting group that met every Tuesday and provided quilts both to seniors in nursing homes and for premature babies in the neonatal units at both Baptist and Forsyth hospitals.

In March 2001, the Winston-Salem community experienced another opportunity that grew out of the relationships that began in the Dialogue. Bertha Roundtree and her daughter, Charlene Thompson, from Grace chose to use the medium of movies and documentaries to foster communication around difficult issues in the community. Their first movie was *Bonhoeffer: Agent of Grace* that invited people to reflect on the themes of discipleship and forgiveness. While supported by the Dialogue, the movie group was independent and open to all members of the Winston-Salem area.

This group continued under Bertha and Charlene's leadership for several years, providing movies that addressed controversial subjects in the areas of sexuality, homophobia, racism, corporate greed, classism, healthcare, etc. Each movie was followed by discussion led by a facilitator and often a panel of experts on the subject. In 2003, they showed such movies as *Nothing But a Man, Twelve Angry Men, Corapeake, Stones of Ibarra, Sins of the Fathers, Gender revolution, and Escape From Affluenza.* It provided a safe place for members from all parts of the community to engage in conversation around subjects where the ethical boundaries were increasingly fluid.

A third movement that was stimulated by the relationships that were formed in the Dialogue was in the area of music. Frequently, as the Dialogue churches gathered for worship, singers from the various churches would join together to offer an anthem. Their musical talents increased their friendships. In 2008, The Reverend Stevenson asked his Music Director James D. Smith to plan a concert series as a way of providing music programs to the community that otherwise many could not afford to attend. The series began in July, 2008, with an offering of Negro spirituals. Dr. Smith invited members of the other congregations to participate. Out of that experience, Dr. Smith formed *The Voices of God's Children* that consisted of about forty singers who desired to give witness to God's love and grace through singing together. They sang spirituals, anthems, and hymns, both accompanied and a cappella. Their debut concert took place on November 16 at Highland Presbyterian. Consistent with the mission of the Dialogue, they asked attendees to bring non-perishable food items for the Second Harvest Food Bank. Later the Voices of God's Children expanded beyond people in the Dialogue churches and now includes many members from around the community.

The VOGC experienced the tragic death of their founder, James Daniel Smith, but he had laid the foundation which would not be denied. By 2012, in a memorial concert in memory of Mr. Smith, it was recognized that already they had offered twenty- five concerts around the Piedmont Triad. Their choir consists of people from twenty different religious and non-religions organizations. They are dedicated to the preservation of the historic music of the African-American community.

Throughout the twenty years of the Dialogue, the relationships formed provided the impetus for a number of collaborative events. In 2001, under the direction of Sue Baker, the parish nurse at Trinity, the Dialogue supported holding a Health Fair for all interested parties. In February 2001, Jonathan Freeman, Associate Pastor at Parkway, conducted a multiple week Grief Support group.

On November 9, 2005, members of Lloyd, Grace, and Highland

boarded a bus to D'iberville, Mississippi. They worked on debris removal and damage assessment following Hurricane Katrina. Several of the churches also provided support for families displaced by the storm who were living in Winston-Salem. A unique addition to the Dialogue's response to this disaster was to convene an interfaith, interracial meeting of the youth with representatives from the Mosque, Temple, and Christian congregations guiding the discussion on how our various faiths provided us guidance on how to respond in times of tragedy and disaster. It may have been the only tri-faith youth discussion of such a nature that has ever been held. It was made possible because the congregations had already formed a foundation of strong relationships.

In 2010, when the tragedy struck Haiti, one member church, Parkway, already had strong connections with Haiti through fourteen years of mission trips. The Dialogue responded by committing $1,500 for assistance and $500 to support Dr. Tom Spangler who, on January 26 traveled to Leogane to provide medical assistance with several other doctors from Winston-Salem on January 26. Later, Parkway organized an additional trip in which members of the dialogue participated. In 2011, the Dialogue sponsored a *Spring for Haiti* outdoor benefit at Lloyd. Through music, food, and fellowship, the Dialogue raised $13,000 from about 300 participants. This money was directed to places of need in Haiti because of all the previous work and relationships that Parkway Presbyterian had built. The connectional church was made visible in a ministry in Winston-Salem that was able to reach out and touch people in Haiti who were also part of the Body of Christ.

Another event that gave expression to the worldwide community of Christ occurred on September 21, 2010. This day had been designated the International Day of Peace. Building on the initiative of Laura Spangler and Lloyd Church, the PIRD churches co-sponsored a Peace Fair and invited David LaMotte, a well-known singer and storyteller, to be their featured speaker. They also invited community groups from around Winston-Salem to set up food booths representing the many cultures around the city. Over 250 citizens of Winston-Salem came and enjoyed the taste of our diverse world cultures living in Winston-Salem.

One of the special developments in Winston-Salem that did not grow out of the Dialogue but for which the Dialogue was especially prepared to participate was the establishment of the Institute for Dismantling Racism. In 2004, the Reverend Willard Bass, a recent graduate from Wake Forest Divinity School, received a grant from the Z. Smith Reynolds Foundation to establish a new organization, the *Winston-Salem Institute for Dismantling Racism.* Its purpose was to educate, organize, and support people to develop anti-racist identity, culture, and institutions to end oppression. A major focus of their efforts was to provide a two and one-half day training session conducted by the Crossroads Ministry in Chicago, Illinois for as many members in Winston-Salem as possible. The Dialogue voted to become partners with IDR and to provide partial scholarships so that they could have participants from all six congregations participating. By May of 2005, more than 100 people from Winston-Salem had participated in the training including 20 people from the Dialogue churches, the most of any agency in Winston-Salem.

ONE FAMILY AT A TIME

CHAPTER 8

S ometimes the best way to build community among those who have experienced division is to join together in looking beyond yourself. Which would make you feel better—winning a debate with someone or joining with them to help a third person who is clearly in need? In the study experiences and shared social events, the Dialogue was tearing down strangerhood. They also chose to join together to make the world a better place. Since a major emphasis of the Dialogue was the building of community, they looked for ways that members could work on projects together. They recognized the impact on a person's dignity and security of having a home of their own. Therefore, they began to look for possibilities in connection with Habitat for Humanity.

Habitat for Humanity, which was expanding its efforts in Forsyth County, provided the Dialogue an opportunity to reach out and build community one family at a time. In 1994, about two years after the Dialogue began, they encouraged members to volunteer during a Habitat build. In September, 1996, Dr. Charles Gunn, a member from Highland, expanded this effort by choosing the Habitat Labor Day Blitz as an opportunity to make the Dialogue effort more visible. He chose the slogan, HELP, Habitat Engages Loving Presbyterians. Habitat constructed a sign outside of one of the houses recognizing the Dialogue's special participation.

Sometimes in building community, you reach out to others and discover that you have also helped your own. In 1995, as the Dialogue continued their efforts, they were rewarded to learn that Ava Bethea, a member of Grace, was going to be the recipient of one of the houses.

During the twenty years of the Dialogue's existence, its member churches celebrated significant anniversaries of their own. Fiftieth anniversaries were celebrated by Highland in 1999 and Dellabrook in 2006 and Trinity in 2009. Centennial anniversaries were celebrated by Grace in 2007 and Parkway in 2012. Lloyd celebrated its 125th anniversary in 1999.

Celebrating anniversaries often generate new opportunities. As Highland was approaching her fiftieth anniversary, a planning task force determined that it was consistent with their faith that part of that celebration should contribute to others both nationally and internationally. They decided to raise money for a project in Guatemala and to build a Habitat house locally.

Because of the relationships built in the last seven years with the Dialogue churches, they invited these churches to join them in the build. In addition, because of their friendship with their neighbor, Temple Emanuel, they also invited the Jewish congregation to participate. Because of a friendship Steve had with a local Imam, it seemed good to invite them to participate as well. Betty Jones, a member of the task force, and Sue Kent, a Highland member came to the Dialogue and presented the proposal.

They did not know it at the time, but they later discovered that they were the first build in the world to be sponsored by three faiths and two races. In 2,000, the local Habitat agency would be awarded the Habitat International Clarence Jordon award for creativity and innovation.

Once the Dialogue made the commitment, they made plans to augment Highlands anniversary fund to arrive at the $50,000 required to build a house. The youth from the six churches gathered together to paint signs to invite people to two different car washes that raised almost $700. Then the Dialogue planned a yard sale at Parkway Presbyterian and were ecstatic when that event raised $6,000 towards the build. This was added to the anniversary fund raised by Highland and a Grant from WS Foundation to promote such builds of diversity to complete the necessary funds for this first Dialogue build.

Then came 9/11 with all the fears and suspicions that the event created. The Dialogue was aware that in addition to the racial divisions that they were seeking to heal, there was also a rising fear among world religions. In Winston-Salem there were two Muslim Communities and a Jewish community. How would you counter such fears in the community?

The Dialogue decided to build on what they did best. Remember the Dialogue began by talking. First, they issued a letter of concern warning against acts of hate and fear.

The events of September 11 and afterward boggle our minds and break our hearts. We are filled with grief, anger, and fear. Yet we have hope.

As pastors and educators of the Presbyterian Inter-racial Dialogue of Winston-Salem, we have had some experience of working alongside and seeking to understand people of others races and faith communities. Our faith encourages respect for persons of other faith traditions and deplores stereotyping and extremist responses to people who are different. We affirm the peace potential of all major religious faiths. . . Although it may not seem popular or practical at the moment, we believe that war is not the way to lasting peace, that there are better alternatives to bombs and bullets, that our nation and all others must explore the root causes of hatred and terrorism, and that God is bigger than the policies or practices of any one nation."

Then, knowing how community is strengthened by working together, the Dialogue chose to sponsor another Habitat build, making sure that the Muslim community was a full participant. Many of those who had participated in the last build were eager to rejoin the effort. In addition, many new members volunteered. The witness was of black, white, and Christian, Jew, and Muslim working together to counter the voice of hate. In future builds, the new Hispanic Presbyterian church and a second Muslim community would join in the builds. The youth of the three faith communities also worked together, including offering a very successful dinner/talent show that both raised money and displayed the multiple talents of the youth across our community.

In the 2006 build, it was determined to ask each of the congregations to organize a fund raising effort that included all the congregations. One of those events was a golf tournament and silent auction on May 15, 2005. Guest speakers and honorary co-chairmen for the event were Jim Grobe, head foot-ball coach at Wake Forest and Kermit Blount, head football coach of Winston-Salem State.

Lloyd, Grace, and Dellabrook planned a cookout on August 27. Then on September 24 Parkway again hosted the very successful yard sale. The youth held a silent auction at Trinity in November and a Dinner and Talent show in January.

As the Dialogue plus their partners from the Jewish and Muslim communities continued to work together, they discovered new friendships and new ways to express the commonalities of their faiths while still respecting the integrity of each congregation's distinctions. The last two builds, 2010 and 2012 added a new feature in that they raised the additional money to build "green" houses or energy efficient houses. In the culminating celebration of the 2010 build held at Temple Emanuel, they chose to eat on dishes and wash them together afterwards as an expression of their environmental commitment.

Under the coordinating hand of Sue Kent of Highland, each build surfaced unique leadership from the several communities. Two events perhaps symbolized the special efforts of these unique builds. First, Orlando and Dennis James, the new resident of the 2010 unity build were a Muslim family. It was a strong counter-voice to the violent voice raised on 9/11 and the voices of fear and hatred that cried out for vengeance.

Second, in May of 2010, the Winston Salem Foundation awarded Sue Kent, who had coordinated the four builds up to that time, the Echo Award for her efforts in contributing to the development of Social Capital in our community. Pastors from all three faiths wrote glowing letters of recommendation on her behalf.

Imam Irshad Hasan wrote, "In the preamble to our constitution it is stated, 'we are endowed by our Creator with certain inalienable rights among those life, liberty and the pursuit of happiness.' . . .Sue Kent has been a staunch advocate for this right through her marvelous work and effort with Habitat for Humanity. Her dedication and infectious energy and enthusiasm has kept those of us at Masjid Al-Mu'minun motivated to continue to help in this most noble cause. . ."

Rabbi Mark Strauss-Cohn wrote, "It is with great honor and pleasure that I endorse the nomination of Sue Kent for an ECHO award. Sue works tirelessly on behalf of the interfaith and inter-racial partnership which we have created to build four Habitat for Humanity homes here in Forsyth County. She believes deeply in the projects. She approaches the volunteers, clergy, and build-family all with respect and humility. She understands how these projects help to build social, emotional and spiritual capital in all the participants . . ."

Each of the pastors of the Protestant churches wrote equally appreciative letters of support.

In presenting the award at the Winston-Salem Foundation banquet at the Benton Convention Center, the following was said about Sue's work:

Sue Kent has built bridging social capital by bringing together diverse racial and religious community members to participate in four Habitat for Humanity house builds over nine years. As coordinator of the first build in 2000, Sue led six Christian churches (including three predominantly African-American and three predominantly white congregations), the Jewish temple and the Muslim mosque to plan and build a Habitat House together. This 2000 build was later awarded the Clarence E. Jordan Award from Habitat International as the first such interfaith and interracial build in the nation. For the second build in 2002, joint fundraisers, including a youth-led talent night, and a unity walk were added, and subsequent builds occurred in 2006 and 2009. In her quiet, gracious, and persistent way, Sue has helped to build trust between and awareness of the enriching variety of faiths and races in Winston-Salem as so many worked together to help families achieve their goals of home ownership.

Sue continued her efforts in coordinating the fifth build in celebration of the twentieth anniversary of PIRD. At the dedication of this fifth house, Jose Quinonez from Habitat for Humanity International in Washington D.C. joined with the six pastors, and representatives from the Jewish community and both Muslim communities in Winston-Salem to welcome the latest resident to her new home.

Ten years after the first of these five inter-racial, interfaith builds was completed, Sue Kent and Gary Simes, an elder at Highland, returned to speak with the first resident, Gloria Cole. Gloria's dream had been to be an in-home childcare provider. She has received her Bachelor of Science degree in childcare. Over the past ten years, she has had up to seventeen children at once over three shifts in a day. Last year she was nominated for the Smart Start Child care Teacher of the year in Forsyth County and was one of three teachers to win. Her son now lives in Burlington and her granddaughter, nearly 18, has begun classes at the Art Institute in Charlotte on full scholarship.

Wayne Linville, an elder from Parkway and a frequent coordinator of the construction crews for the builds, accompanied Sue Kent in visiting the owners of the second house built. Mia Anthony and her 3-year-old son, Ojie, moved in eight years ago. Today Mia works at Time Warner Cable as an Administrative Assistant and is planning on getting her Masters in Information Technology, and maybe someday, even pursue a law degree.

Similar stories are told about the other residents. They are stories of people's lives that have been changed one home at a time for one family at a time. This is what can happen when people who have been divided by their differences in society come together and look beyond themselves to respond to the needs of others.

The years of working together on Habitat builds have become a good metaphor for the Dialogue. In addition to reaching across racial divisions, they have found themselves reaching across generational divisions, religious divisions, and class divisions. Sometimes you start small with a conversation. At other times, you stand up and give voice to your protest against an injustice or advocate for a community improvement. Then you find yourself reaching out to a single family who wants to find a home in their community. You try to prevent racism and prejudice from hurting your neighbor and you discover that you experience healing in your own soul.

SHARING A MEAL

CHAPTER 9

The Bible is filled with stories of important events that happen while people are sharing a meal. From the celebration of the Passover meal to the Lord's Supper, meals have been central to the faith journey. It was when Abram prepared a meal for three strangers at the Oak of Moreh that God appeared to him and the journey began. At the time, Abram was not aware of all that was going to happen on that journey.

I offer that to you, the reader, as background for what happens when you share meals together on a journey of faith. There were many meals that were shared in the past twenty years of the Inter-racial Dialogue. Frequently food was at the center of the gathering of clergy, the whole Dialogue, and either during or following worship. Food was also at the center of our gathering of the inter-faith group that built the Habitat homes.

It is a strange thing about sharing a meal together. You can never be quite sure of what will happen. That is amplified if you continue to share on a regular basis. For almost 18 years, Sam Stevenson and Steve McCutchan shared breakfast together twice a month at the same restaurant. For most of those years, they had the same waitress, Debbie. They shared personal stories of agony and joy. There were times when each were experiencing pain and the other was there to support. There were times when each had personal joys in the family or career and the other one was there to celebrate. Like Abram, they could not have anticipated the variety of events, challenges, idea, and pleasures that first surfaced during those conversations at breakfast.

69

They wanted to deepen their friendship with full recognition that the implications of race and their respective histories shaped by their different races affected all that they experienced. They did not want to arrive at a friendship where race did not matter. As they deepened their friendship, they grew in their ability to explore the effect of race on their lives without defensiveness, allowing the wounds to be exposed with less fear. They also experienced the joy of benefiting from their differences and wanted to offer that same blessing to others.

It was probably in 1997, about three years after they began sharing breakfast together, that a new idea was born. They were looking for a way to deepen their friendship and to share the benefits of that with others. What resources would you turn to in such a situation?

Because they were both Christians, they sought the resources of their faith to assist them. This led to a conversation about how their race contributed to what they heard when they read Scripture. They knew that no one reads Scripture from an objective perspective. A comfortably wealthy person reads the parable of the Pharisee and the tax collector praying in the temple (Luke 18:9) differently than a person who has been harshly judged by society. They began to talk about how we read Scripture from a racial perspective.

This led to looking at the Peter / Cornelius story in Acts 10 and particularly how that might sound differently to a white person than it would to a black person. As they discussed this, it occurred to them that they might present their understanding to others in the form of a play. It took them a couple of years and numerous drafts before they came up with a play based on Acts 10. During their conversation, Sam recalled that he had preached a sermon on this text at a five church interracial worship service when he was a pastor in Wilson, North Carolina. He had titled the sermon, "That Great Family Reunion," and that became the title of their play.

They set their goal to prepare the play and recruit the actors in time for an anniversary celebration at Grace Presbyterian on May 21, 1999. Since neither of them had ever written a play before, they also learned during the process that it was all right to experience frustration and even some anger at each other during the process. Once the written form of the play was complete, they had to gather about 30 people, including a combined choir for the performance. They were fortunate to find Nell Britton to direct the play. For over 20 years, she had directed theater at Reynolds High School and had formed her own dinner theater group.

This performance was followed by a repeat performance at Highland Presbyterian on November 12, 1999. Members of the other Dialogue churches were invited to both performances.

Two and one-half years later, the Presbyterian Women of Salem Presbytery were having their 15th annual Spring Gathering and they invited the cast to present *That Great Family Reunion* as a kick off to their year of study focused on "No Longer Strangers, United in Christ."

In March of 2003, Salem Presbytery held a Diversity II conference at Camp Hanes and the cast of *That Great Family Reunion* was invited to perform. After the performance, the moderator of that event wrote, "The talent and work required to put on such a professionally done drama is awesome. . .My wife had the privilege of seeing an earlier performance done for an area wide "Women of the Church" group to which she gave an excellent review. . .The message of your play was clear and direct. It fit in perfectly with the goal of our conference to celebrate and to encourage diversity within our presbytery and world. It represents a most powerful worship experience."

To provide you, the reader, with a sense of the play, the outline of the cast and an excerpt from scene 5 is included. Since it took almost 30 people from the two congregations to present the play, you can see the tremendous commitment it took from the two congregations.

Casting for Play

From Sam's Congregation
     Need 8 to 10 people
From Steve's Congregation
     Need 8 – 10 people
For Peter's Vision, need following individuals all dressed in rags
     A white person depicting a street walker

A black addict
A white alcoholic
A black convict
A white mobster type
A white beggar
A black elderly (maybe handicapped)
A black child
A white flower child
A white waitress
An angel (liturgical dancer)
A Narrator
A voice of God
A soldier under Cornelius
2 servants of Cornelius
Peter will be played by Steve
Cornelius will be played by Sam
A choir of 4 to 8 black members and 4-8 white members

Scene 5: Peter's House

Narrator

About noon the next day, as the messengers from Cornelius were on their journey and approaching the city, Peter went apart by himself to pray:

(The Scene focuses on a lone Peter kneeling in prayer. While he is kneeling, it is not a humble kneeling but the type of posture of one who is used to being in charge. His head is thrown back and he is looking up as he prays and his voice is confident as if he is in a conversation with an equal.)

Peter

God, I want to thank you for helping me heal that young Tabitha yesterday. That is certainly the type of power that is going to get people's attention and let them know that we have the truth on our side.

Voice (from off stage)

Who has the truth and power, Peter?

Peter

(Somewhat startled to actually hear a voice)
"Lord, is that you? I didn't know you were there. I mean I knew you were there, I just didn't expect you to respond. I mean I knew you would respond, I just didn't expect to hear you. Well, that isn't what I mean either.

Lord. I clearly recognize that the truth and power belong to you. But I am grateful that you have led me to this new understanding. Without your help, I would be like these other religious hypocrites who keep mouthing the words but not understanding the truth about Jesus.

Voice

And what is that truth, Peter.

Peter

That Jesus is the Christ and Lord of all. And that all people will come to this truth and know the shalom that you have intended from the beginning.

(Peter has been so focused on his conversation with God that he doesn't see that a series of people are starting to walk down the aisle towards him. There is a whole procession, first a flower child begging and trying to sell flowers for a little money in her tin can. Next a streetwalker with heavy makeup, short skirt, lots of cheap jewelry and swinging her purse. Followed by a Drug Addict preparing to get a fix, an alcoholic stumbling down with his bottle, an elderly woman who is crippled and barely able to walk, a hip hopper complete with boom box and jeans hung low, an escaped convict complete with ball and chain, and a mobster type in long black coat, white tie, and black hat.

Voice

Look around you Peter. Invite my people to dine with you this day.
(Peter looks and sees clearly that this group of people is not from his own kind. They are of different class, races, and economic stations in life. All of them would make either congregation uncomfortable.)

Peter

Lord, these are clearly the riffraff that are destroying our world.

Voice

See that child selling flowers, Peter, let her know that she has someone to watch over her.
(Peter rises and walks around some of the different people, making an almost exaggerated display of not touching or being touched by any of them.)

Peter

Isn't that disgusting, Lord. Imagine parents sending a helpless child like that out into the streets to beg. I'll bet they use the money for drugs. You should give them a piece of your mind, Lord.

Voice

And what about that man lying at your door step. Can't you help him out of his drunken haze.

Peter

Lord, if I let him in the church, half the congregation would get drunk on the smell. This is a test, isn't it, Lord. You want to see if I'm really committed. I know I kept some bad company in the past, but I only associate with people of the Way now. I'm completely committed to building your church.

Voice

And what about that woman who walks with a cane, can't she still make a contribution to humanity?

Peter

She's old Lord. Were trying to build a church. That will take lots of people with energy and resources. She is past her day. When we get the church built, then we will take care of her Lord.

Voice

Show that young hip hopper your commitment by giving him some guidance for his future.

Peter

Someone needs to give him some guidance, that's for sure. Doesn't that music offend your ears? We want good music in the church, Lord. And look at those pants. There so low they hardly cover his ankles.

Voice

And what about that convict, Peter, doesn't he need forgiveness?

Peter

He's an escaped convict, Lord. You are a God of justice aren't you. He needs to pay his debt to society and then we will receive him into the church.

Voice

Put your arm around that streetwalker, Peter. Tell her you know what society has done to her. Tell her she is welcome among God's people.

Peter

Lord, my Lord, if I brought her to worship the Jerusalem council would have my head. I know we are to be forgiving, Lord. Your son taught us that. But she would have to demonstrate that she has repented first.

Voice

And what about that addict, Peter who is seeking salvation through mainlining a drug.

Peter

Well, you know what they say about drug addicts, Lord. "Lock those druggies up till they get well. Otherwise they will go straight to ___--well, you know what I mean, Lord.

Voice

And that fellow over there (indicating the mobster). You've seen him associating with the worst criminals in town, Peter, does he belong?

Peter

Looks like a Samaritan to me Lord. They have compromised their faith so badly; it would take a miracle to straighten them out. Some day, Lord, but we can't move too fast or it will destroy your church.

Voice

Peter, these are my church. What God has made clean, you must not call profane.

(Peter stands in shock while the people one by one come by him, touch or hug him, and slowly leave the sanctuary.)

(As they leave the hidden choir sings *In Christ There Is No East or West*

The play, the experience in writing it, producing it, and performing it several times was a demanding experience. Yet it was fulfilling also as it continued to expand the mission of the Dialogue.

It was also a reminder that you need to be careful when you sit down to eat a meal with someone. You never know what can emerge.

CELEBRATING THE CONVERSATION

CHAPTER 10

"Come now, let us reason together, says the LORD: though your sins are like scarlet, they shall be as white as snow; though they are red like crimson, they shall become like wool." (Isaiah 1:18 [RSV])

This is the story of The Presbyterian Inter-racial Dialogue of Winston-Salem, North Carolina. While it started small and has never sought a lot of publicity, it has been recognized both locally and nationally for its efforts to bridge the divisions of our world.

On April 30, 2001, the Forsyth chapter of Habitat for Humanity was one of only two to receive Habitat International's Clarence Jordan Award for creativity and innovation in honor of the inter-racial, inter-faith build by the Dialogue churches. This was the first habitat build in the world that involved Christians, Muslims, and Jews and African Americans and Caucasians.

In 2001, the City of Winston-Salem Human Relations Commission awarded the Dialogue Churches and their Jewish and Muslim colleagues with the Faith Award for their contribution to the Winston-Salem Community. The Commission presents such awards to the individual, or group "who exhibit outstanding achievements in furthering human rights and equal opportunity in Winston-Salem through advocacy, action, and education."

Also in 2001, the *Seguaro Seminar* by the John F. Kennedy School of Government at Harvard University issued a report *bettertogether* in which the inter-racial, interfaith build by the Dialogue churches and the Jewish and Muslim community was cited as an example for the nation on "overcoming incivility distrust, animosity, and sometimes even violence" in our society.

In 2002, the Winston-Salem Foundation, in offering their second year of social capital, ECHO (Everyone Can Help Out) awards said the following, **"The Rev. Sam Stevenson & Rev. Steve McCutchan** were nominated as a 'social capital building team' who share a deep and abiding friendship and collegiality. Willing to be leaders when few were following, they helped to create the Presbyterian Interracial Dialogue, now in its 10th year. It has become a thriving force for community reconciliation, education, and many new friendships. Together they have promoted integrated schools, the police review board, and more than their share of informal socializing—particularly when food is involved. Recently they co-wrote a play that was performed by their two churches. Sam and Steve were nominated by Rev. Laura Spangler of Lloyd Presbyterian Church.

In 2004, at the 216th General Assembly of the Presbyterian Church (USA), the Dialogue was awarded the Restorative Justice Award. This award was established in 1991 "to recognize Presbyterians individuals or groups related to the Presbyterian Church (U.S.A.) who are making outstanding contributions to direct-service ministries or to change advocacy in the criminal justice system. The principle of restorative justice is addressing the hurts and needs of the victims, the offender, and the community in such a way that all might be healed."

Then in 2010, as mentioned in the chapter 8, Sue Kent received another Echo Award from the Winston-Salem Foundation for guiding the first four Interfaith, Inter-racial builds in the city. As was mentioned, after the award, she proceeded to guide the fifth build as part of our celebration of PIRD's 20th anniversary.

Such recognition, while appreciated, was not the main purpose of the Dialogue. The purpose was always to build community where it was broken. For the first eight years, that effort was primarily directed by the clergy of the six churches. With the exception of the financial commitments to the Habitat builds, the churches had not been asked to make financial contributions towards a PIRD budget. Then in November of 2,000, representatives of the Dialogue churches met with Mike Warren of the Salem Presbytery staff to explore the formation of a council made up of both clergy and elder representatives of each church.

This was prompted by two developments. One was the possibility, which became a reality, of the hiring of Clarisse Durnell to work with both the Dialogue and their African American churches. The second development was the recognition that three of the clergy that had been providing the leadership for the Dialogue would be retiring within a few years. With this change in pastoral leadership among several of the churches, the stability of the Dialogue would be enhanced if it had a council of church representatives and an institutional structure.

In January 2001, the council officially formed. Their first act was to confirm the financial commitment of each of the churches towards Clarisse's salary. They also prepared a covenant agreement that each church was asked to examine and affirm. Based on the initial mission statement that the Dialogue had been using, it asked each church to commit to:

1. Electing members of our session who will serve the **PIRD** Council.
2. Making available the use of church facilities for worship, fellowship, and PIRD meetings.
3. Contributing to **PIRD**'s financial needs as approved by the Session.
4. Encouraging and supporting **PIRD**'s staff.
5. Promoting and engaging in common ministry.

It was a significant step towards a recognition of the oneness of the Body of Christ and each church's individual part in it. At that time they also developed a pattern of alternating the chair of the council both between lay and ordained members and between black and white churches.

PIRD moved from being a movement among the churches to

becoming an institution of the church. Later, as they would look back on it, this had benefits and costs. One of the costs was that the clergy no longer met regularly, which had been a major factor in the development of their relationship. The benefit was that the officers of the respective churches became more aware and involved in this ministry. An important event in this development was a banquet on October 25, 2002, for the officers of all three churches to celebrate the history of the Dialogue and to envision its future.

It is time to celebrate coming together for the conversation. It is time to acknowledge that none of us is pure but we are enriched by our relationships with those who are different from us. It is time to recognize that as we overcome our fear of those who are different we are preparing ourselves to relate to God who is totally different from all of us. It is time to praise God who has provided us a world of rich diversity. It is time to reflect the image of God who created this world in all its beauty and called it "very good." (Genesis 1:31)

For twenty years, we have been given the privilege of working together as two races, black and white, and over time being able to reach out to our Hispanic neighbors and our Jewish and Muslim communities. We have learned of each other's pain, been confronted by the guilt of our history, and enriched by the promise of a truly multi-cultural world. Sometimes we participated enthusiastically and sometimes grudgingly, but when one of us faltered, there was another brother or sister who took our place. We have learned to reason together without being defensive about the truth that our sins are like scarlet. We share in the worship of a God who is not defeated by our sins, past or present, and who has shown us as God told Paul, "My grace is sufficient for you, for my power is made perfect in weakness." (2 Corinthians 12:9)

The future for the Dialogue, as we celebrate twenty years, is ambiguous and continually evolving. Yet, like with Abram, that is sort of the way it is when you are on a journey of faith. However, if you have read this far, then you too are part of the Dialogue. I would ask you what you are willing to do to contribute to the healing of this world, especially that part of it divided by race, religion, and ethnicity. Before you say to yourself, "I'm concerned but I don't have any idea where to start," I would remind you that this whole twenty-year journey began with three people having lunch. Strange and amazing things happen when you take the time to share food with someone and open yourself to the possibilities.

So I would ask you, "Who are you going to take to lunch?"

(Conclude with another poem by RaVanda written in celebration of this anniversary.)